Perl Debugged

Perl Debugged

Peter Scott and Ed Wright

ADDISON-WESLEY

Boston ♦ San Francisco ♦ New York ♦ Toronto ♦ Montreal
London ♦ Munich ♦ Paris ♦ Madrid
Capetown ♦ Sydney ♦ Tokyo ♦ Singapore ♦ Mexico City

Contents

Perlness

In the world of languages, the country of Perl is the great melting pot which welcomes all cultures, religions, and beliefs. "Give me your tired, your poorly-supported programmers, your huddled masses yearning to be free of artificial limitations," says Perl, and those who land on its shores find an environment where they are no longer hampered by a language designer's whimsical notions of elegant semantics and stifling syntactical purity.

Perl's universal availability and ease-of-use make it the most democratic programming language. Unlike many other languages, a relative beginner can write useful programs, whereas effective programmers in other languages normally need to spend a lot longer to learn syntax, operators, and functions. A Perl programmer may possess such expertise, or may be a newcomer who modified some example script to perform a new function.

But the newcomer has another problem: lack of debugging skills. Experience forces the canny to develop an innate knack for debugging due to years of accumulated pain. We want to minimize that pain, because we have suffered it. Perl's ease of use allows programmers with little knowledge to create usable, if fragile, code. The amount of time it takes to debug a Perl program can vary dramatically from person to person. Our goal is to help you minimize the development, debugging, and maintenance time you need for your own Perl programs.

Do not take the title of this book to imply we are debugging Perl itself in these pages. What few bugs exist in the Perl interpreter are a matter of minute exotica (or exotic minutiae), rapidly squashed by the fine volunteer crew supporting Perl. A more accurate title would have been *Debugging Your Perl Programs*, but that felt too pedestrian and loses the "unplugged" pun.

We wrote this book because we wanted you to see the development process at work. Most books on programming contain carefully crafted examples honed through sweaty practice to work perfectly and stand as mute testimonial to the elegant style of the author. They don't show you the ugly, irritating process it took to get the examples into shape; yet those examples did not in fact spring into existence fully formed from the forehead of their creator. Because you will experience this same process when developing your programs, we want to guide you through it and describe various ways around the embarrassment, humiliation, and surprising pitfalls that stand between you and Great Programming.

Within this book, we describe the most common and annoying mistakes a new Perl programmer might make, and then detail the procedures to identify and correct those bugs and any others. You should have *some* knowledge of Perl; several fine tutorials exist to free us from the onerous responsibility of explaining scalars and arrays and hashes and the like. This preface includes a few references to some of the most useful of these tutorials.

We will not attempt to define or describe a proper programming "style." Style is as unique as an individual—but a few general rules create a common reference so that we can easily read each other's programs.

Neither is this a "how to program" book. Although we will probe into the mechanics and underpinnings of the general principle of programming at times, it is not our intention to inculcate a complete newcomer with the mindset of the programmer's discipline.

Who Are You?

If you've been programming in Perl anywhere from a week to a year and want to speed up your development cycle, this book is for you. We'll also address some issues related to developing in a team. This book is intended to assist those who have started learning Perl by providing practical advice on development practices.

What This Book Covers

Here's what you'll find in the rest of this book:

- *Chapter 1:* Introduction and a guided tour of the Perl documentation

- *Chapter 2:* Developing the right mindset for programming and developing effectively

- *Chapter 3:* "Gotchas" in Perl: Working your way around some of the tricky things to understand or get right in Perl programming

- *Chapter 4:* Antibugging: How to code defensively

- *Chapter 5:* How to instrument your code

- *Chapter 6:* How to test your Perl programs

- *Chapter 7:* A tour of the perl debugger: our guide to using this built-in tool

- *Chapter 8:* Types of syntax error and how to track down their causes

- *Chapter 9:* Run-time errors

- *Chapter 10:* Semantical errors: When your program appears to work but doesn't do the right thing

- *Chapter 11:* How to improve the performance of a resource-hungry (memory, CPU cycles, and so on) program

- *Chapter 12:* Tips and pitfalls for people coming to Perl from other languages

- *Chapter 13:* Common Gateway Interface (CGI) programming: special tips for debugging this type of Perl program

- *Chapter 14:* Conclusion

- *Appendix A:* Reference for the Perl debugger commands

- *Appendix B:* List of our "Perls of Wisdom"

We will spend a lot of time going through examples of problems and how you might debug them.

Getting Perl

While this isn't a book about how to install or build perl,[1] we owe you at least rudimentary instructions on how to get a perl of your own.

- For Windows machines, get the free ActivePerl distribution:

  ```
  http://www.activeState.com/ActivePerl/
  download.htm
  ```

- For Macintoshes:

  ```
  http://www.cpan.org/ports/index.html#mac
  ```

- For binary distributions for all other machines:

  ```
  http://www.cpan.org/ports/
  ```

- For the source of perl itself:

  ```
  http://www.cpan.org/src/
  ```

Building perl from source on a supported Unix architecture requires just these commands after you download and unpack the right file:

```
./Configure
make
make test
make install   # if the make test succeeds
```

The Configure step asks you zillions of questions, and most people won't have a clue what many of those questions are talking about; but the default answers Configure recommends are usually correct.

---

1. That's not a typo. By convention, big-P Perl refers to the language in the abstract, whereas little-p perl refers to the program that runs Perl programs.

For educational purposes, you may want to build a perl that has debugging enabled. (Here we refer to a perl that lets you use the special −D flag to enable the output of information that tells you what perl is doing with your program. This has nothing to do with Perl's built-in interactive debugger—which we discuss in Chapter 7—all perls have that.) If you want to do that, build perl from the source, and when `Configure` asks, "`Any additional cc flags?`" paste in whatever it already shows between brackets as a default and add "`-DDEBUGGING`". See the `perlrun` POD page (explained later) for more information.

We occasionally refer to modules that are not part of the core Perl distribution but that can be found on the Comprehensive Perl Archive Network (CPAN). For instructions on how to find, download, and install a module from CPAN, see `http://www.cpan.org/misc/cpan-faq.html`.

Typographical Conventions

We use the following conventions in this book:

- Standard text: Times Roman
- Author's comments: Arial
- Code examples and URLs: `Courier`
- User input: **`bold Courier`**

Sometimes our code examples have line breaks where none existed in the original. In places where these line breaks would cause problems or aren't obvious, we've put a backslash (\) at the end of the line to indicate that the line should be joined with the next one.

Occasionally, we want you to know which of us is talking to you, so we have this style of comment to let you know. (This is Ed, by the way.)

 Those marginal icons are part of the terrific artwork created by my wife's sister, Ann Palmer, for this book. (This is Peter, by the way.)

For Further Reference

Visit this book's Web site at `http://www.perldebugged.com`.

Get introductions to Perl programming from the following (in rough order of usefulness):

- *Learning Perl,* 2nd ed., by Randal Schwartz and Tom Christiansen (O'Reilly & Associates, 1997)
- *Programming Perl,* 3rd ed., by Larry Wall, Tom Christiansen, and Jon Orwant (O'Reilly & Associates, 2000)
- *Perl, the Programmer's Companion,* by Nigel Chapman (John Wiley & Sons, 1998)
- *Elements of Programming with Perl,* by Andrew Johnson (Manning Publications, 1999)
- *Effective Perl Programming,* by Joseph Hall with Randal Schwartz (Addison-Wesley, 1998)

Perl Versions

In this book, we refer to the latest "stable" version of Perl, which is 5.6.0 as of this writing. The vast majority of what we say works unaltered on older versions of Perl 5, but not Perl 4. If you use any version of Perl older than 5.004_04, you should upgrade; 5.003 had issues such as security problems and memory leaks. You can find out the version number of your perl by passing it the −v flag:

```
% perl -v
This is perl, v5.6.0 built for i586-linux
Copyright 1987-2000, Larry Wall
[...]
```

Perl won't execute a script named on the command line if the −v flag is present. A more detailed description of your perl's configuration can be obtained with the −V flag; if you issue a bug report, the facility for doing that automatically includes this information with your report.[2]

A separate development track exists for Perl; you will know if you have one of those versions because the release number either contains an underscore followed by a number of 50 or larger or contains an odd number between two dots. Nothing is guaranteed to work in such a distribution; it's intended for testing. If you find you have one and you didn't want it, the person who downloaded your perl probably visited the wrong FTP link.

It was announced at the fourth annual Perl Conference (Monterey, California, July 2000) that Perl *6* development was beginning in earnest, and backward compatibility need not stand in the way of doing good things. As of press time, discussion continues on new language features.

---

2. Using the perlbug program included with your perl distribution.

Acknowledgments

 I would like to thank David Noble for the original version of the `proxylog` tool and Ilya Zakharevich for educating me on the intricacies of the Perl debugger. My greatest thanks go to my wife Grace for her love and support through this intensely busy time.

 As always, thanks to my grandmother, Mrs. Charles D. Wright Sr., who let me play with computers and read Doc Savage books, and to Mary O'Brien, who originally approached me about this project.

In addition, we both thank our editor, Mike Hendrickson, and his colleagues, Julie Debaggis and Marcy Barnes, for their tireless support, patience, and understanding while they took a risk on two newcomers to the field and gently ushered us into the fold of authordom. Among the rest of the tireless and often anonymous cast at Addison-Wesley we thank Cathy Comer, Mary Cotillo, Jacquelyn Doucette, John Fuller, Karin Hansen, Katie Noyes, Heather Olszyk, and Heather Peterson.

Our thanks also go to Elaine Ashton for reviews and screenshots, and to Brad Appleton, Sean M. Burke, Joseph Hall, Jarkko Hietaniemi, Michael G. Schwern, and other reviewers for their insightful and helpful comments, which have improved this book immeasurably. Any remaining errors are in no way attributable to them.

## Chapter 1

Introduction

"Well begun is half done."

Mary Poppins

1.1 Reality

Unfortunately for the programming world (and programmers), software development continues after a project is declared finished (an increasingly arbitrary—and often inaccurate—label). Maintenance and debugging may consume more time than the original coding, particularly because the person responsible for a program's maintenance may not be one of the original programmers. This means we spend a lot of our time trying to deduce the specifics of some algorithm we find in the code: how it was done, why it was done, and why it doesn't work any more.[1]

The odds of creating a bug-free program are rather long. Anything larger than the ubiquitous *Hello World* program is fair game for bugs. No recipe exists that, if followed, eliminates the possibility of bugs, but some practical rules have been developed:

1. Reduce the places where a bug may be introduced. This means incorporating modular design, encapsulation, and unit testing.

2. Identify the bug's pathology. Play detective: what shouldn't happen but does, or does happen but shouldn't?

3. Isolate the bug's location—where do things go south? (This is the reason for the invention of debuggers.)

4. Determine the conditions that cause the bug. What activates it? Why haven't you found it before?

5. Correct the bug—and always retest altered code.

6. How did the bug get in there in the first place? If you made a typo and caught it 5 minutes later on a unit test, that's one thing. If the bug was caused by a logic error and survived to release,

---

1. A seminal work in this respect is *The Mythical Man-Month*, by Fred Brooks (Addison-Wesley, 1995).

you have another problem. Find out how to improve your development process so that any similar bugs are found much sooner.

1.2 Why Perl?

Chances are, if you use Perl you know why you picked it and don't need further proselytizing. But additional ammunition never hurts—if you have to defend Perl up your management chain, well, Perl doesn't have a megamultinational conglomerate to pour zillions of dollars into a marketing campaign[2]—so it falls to users like us to sing its praises in practical ways.

Whenever we have a problem we need to solve with a program, the solution first shows up in our mind, in thought pictures and words, which most development methodologies then have us enunciate as an English (or whatever our native language is) description of an algorithm before ever translating it into code. If the algorithm description were complete and unambiguous, it could be executed by a computer if the computer could understand our phraseology.[3] But no parser yet exists for free-form English algorithm descriptions, so we translate the description into some language a machine *can* comprehend.

Therein lies the rub: an ideal computer language imposes zero overhead on the programmer during implemention of the description. Such a thing doesn't exist, so we want the language that minimizes the overhead. This can vary from task to task—if you're writing a device driver, your best choice is quite likely to remain assembler. If you're writing a graphical user interface, at least part of the problem is probably best attacked with a WYSIWYG editor that creates a layout specification.

---

2. If you think we have a specific example in mind, you're probably right.

3. Of course, in practice, we always discover ambiguities and insufficiencies in the natural language description when we later code it, but this can be viewed as just not writing the description adequately. We suspect this is so common because most of us are impatient to get on with the coding anyway.

When writing a program, you're conscious of its overhead every time you create a requirement on code solely to satisfy the demands of the language but not the problem. For example, in writing C and C++ programs, a frequent example of this is how to allocate memory for dynamic data structures and where and when to give it up.

Perl imposes on the programmer the smallest overhead of any language we have used for the vast majority of problems we have had to solve. At the expense of little learning, we are able to create very short programs in an incredibly brief time to solve complex problems. Because the language overhead is small, changes in requirements don't force changes in large unrelated sections of the code since a much more natural mapping from the English description of the solution to the Perl version exists. And because the Perl expression of the solution is so succinct, a reader can encompass more of it at a glance.

In fact, in many respects, Perl resembles English in its ability to resolve ambiguities favorably, its intuitive and orthogonal interfaces, and even how it sounds when read out loud.[4] Larry Wall, Perl's creator, often states how his background in linguistics led him to consciously draw such parallels.[5] Perl cognoscenti refer to this collective phenomenon as Perl's DWIM (Do What I Mean) behavior.

If you're in need of arguments of the kind that sway managers in favor of Perl, see the *Perl Success Stories* page at `http://perl.oreilly.com/news/success_stories.html`. If you're in need of arguments of the kind that sway scientists, see the language comparison paper by Lutz Prechelt to be found at `http://wwwipd.ira.uka.de/~prechelt/Biblio/jccpprtTR.pdf`.

---

4. We don't know whether this makes Perl easier or harder to learn for nonnative English speakers. A research topic if ever there was one.

5. You can find Larry's exposition on his guiding principles at:

   `http://www.wall.org/~larry/natural.html`.

1.3 Know the Environment

Knowledge of a language includes experience with the practical meanings of errors in different environments. If a Unix program returns the error `segmentation fault` (those of you on other systems may experience this variously as `ABEND`, `%SYSTEM-F-ACCVIO`, or your machine freezing), an experienced programmer will first suspect a memory problem, often the result of a read or write to an array beyond the array bounds. Another Unix error response, `bus error`, often occurs when a subroutine or function call has an improper argument list. Efficient error identification accompanies experience. This book tries to encapsulate experience with errors made writing Perl programs.

1.4 Know the Language

Just as every country has its customs, so does every computer language. We use a language best when we adopt its customs rather than pretend we know better and try to force this new language to fit our old prejudices.

 Years ago, after I had been working on my first mainframe (an ICL 1903T running George III), I was introduced to my second (technically, a minicomputer: a VAX 11/780 running VAX/VMS). I spent some time defining symbols in the new operating system so that I could type the same commands for listing files, etc., I used in the old one. A wiser programmer nearby inquired, "Why would you want to make VMS look like George III?" Anyone who knows the relative power of their respective command line interfaces will appreciate the irony in this.

Find out the common Perl idioms and practice their use. There are generally good reasons why they're common. If nothing else, adopting them will make your code more maintainable since more people will know what it means.

These idioms can range from the simple two-element "open or die":

```
open FH, $file or die "Can't open $file: $!\n";
```

to the mind-boggling (at first sight) Schwartzian Transform:

```
@sorted = map $_->[0],
          sort { $a->[1] <=> $b->[1] }
          map [ $_, sortable_func($_) ]
          @unsorted;
```

The first idiom soon becomes second nature (our fingers now type it by themselves), although on first learning the language one might come up instead with:

```
if (open FH, $file)
    {
    ...
    }
else
    {
    die "Unable to open $file: $!\n"
    }
```

It's not hard to see why the idiom caught on. (Briefly, here's why it works: open returns false if it fails, and the or logical operator is *short-circuiting,* which means it doesn't evaluate its second argument if the first one is true, because the value of A or B is fixed as soon as we know A is true.)

The second idiom provides an efficient way of sorting items that need manipulation before they can be sorted in an "ASCIIbetical" or numeric collating sequence. When you learn this, and realize there are only two tokens in it that can change from one invocation to the next,[6] your eye naturally spots the

---

6. The comparison function can be either <=> or cmp, and the name of the function you provide to turn an unsortable quantity into a sortable one will vary.

`map-sort-map` pattern and translates it to "Schwartzian Transform" whenever appropriate.

1.5 Online Documentation

Fortunately, the documentation included with perl covers practically everything you could want to know about Perl. Unfortunately, practically everything you could want to know about Perl is an awful lot. Yet with a little guidance, you can very quickly learn how to navigate around it and save yourself gobs of time compared to the alternatives. The documentation is in the POD (Plain Old Documentation) format, a very simple markup language that's part of Perl.

Knowing your way around the documentation is an essential debugging tool. Because this is such an important point, we call attention to it with a device we use throughout this book for highlighting such tips, pompously called *Perls of Wisdom:*

 Know the documentation. Be able to find anything in it.

(We have collected all these tips into a list in Appendix B for quick reference.) The most flagrant example of the consequences of ignoring this advice in recent years was the furor over the behavior of the `localtime` function after 1999. Many people looked at the value returned for the year and incorrectly assumed it was formed from the last two digits of the actual year, so they wrote windowing code or just tacked "19" in front of it to get the real year. Unfortunately, according to the Perl documentation,

> ... `$year` is the number of years since 1900, that is, `$year` is `123` in year 2023, and *not* simply the last two digits of the year. If you assume it is, then you create non-Y2K-compliant programs—and you wouldn't want to do that, would you?

As you can tell, some text was added by documenters who were becoming frustrated with the lack of attention this explanation was receiving.

 In 1998 I was called to fix a program I had written over 10 years earlier on a VMS machine that was failing Y2K testing. I was surprised to see I had written windowing code assuming the year returned in a C `tm` struct contained only the last two digits, and as a result the program was printing dates in the year "19100". After I fixed the program, I found the original VMS C manual I had used when writing it, and looked up `localtime`. Lo and behold, it announced that the year field contained the last two digits! (Such a bug would not survive long in Perl's documentation thanks to the open source process controlling it.)

1.5.1 Perl Documentation on Windows

If you're using the ActiveState port of perl for Microsoft Windows, the `perldoc` pages have been converted into pleasantly formatted hyperlinked HTML.[7] You can reach it either through the `Start` button:

```
Programs -> ActivePerl -> Online Documentation
```

or by going to the `html` directory under the root of the installed ActivePerl, and opening the `index.htm` file there. Everything under **Core Perl FAQ**, **Core Perl Docs**, and most of the listings under **Module Docs** are also contained in the standard perl distribution you'll find on any other platform. If you click on **Perl Documentation** in the main frame, you'll be taken to the root of the core documentation for Perl itself rather than the pages created by ActiveState.

This is a good way to browse the documentation, and we quite like this interface. However, browsing isn't enough; you frequently need to pinpoint a

---

7. See the **Getting Perl** section in the Preface for information on how to obtain ActivePerl.

particular section within one of the voluminous sections of documentation. Say you want to find out how to use split; you must go to the giant perlfunc page and scroll down to just the right point. To get around this problem, you can use the command line version, so let's jump into a tour of perldoc.

1.5.2 The perldoc Command

Every system with an installed perl distribution includes perldoc and the files it references. If it doesn't, ask the person who performed the installation to do it again properly. To provide a tool without the documentation to use it properly isn't technically one of the seven deadly sins, but we're lobbying to get it added in their next release.

Just typing perldoc by itself produces little output, but a tantalizing clue:

```
% perldoc
Usage: perldoc [-h] [-r] [-i] [-v] [-t] [-u] [-m] [-l]
[-F] [-X] PageName|ModuleName|ProgramName
        perldoc -f PerlFunc
        perldoc -q FAQKeywords

The -h option prints more help.  Also try "perldoc perldoc" to
get aquainted with the system.
```

This is information on how perldoc itself works, useful if you're trying to find out more about the perldoc program, but not if you're looking for the Perl manuals. If you try either of the suggestions mentioned (perldoc -h or perldoc perldoc), you'll end up only with more verbose information about all the options perldoc can take.

The magic key to unlocking the door to the documents on the Perl language itself is perldoc perl:

```
% perldoc perl
[...]
        For ease of access, the Perl manual has been split up
        into a number of sections:
```

```
perl              Perl overview (this section)
perldelta         Perl changes since previous version
perl5005delta     Perl changes in version 5.005
perl5004delta     Perl changes in version 5.004
perlfaq           Perl frequently asked questions
[...]
```

Bingo! All the different sections you can peruse with `perldoc` are laid out before you, which leads us to our second Perl of Wisdom:

② To get started with the perl documentation, type `perldoc perl`.

The reason it's this way is that a behind-the-scenes equivalence exists between the `perldoc` sections and Unix manual pages. On Unix systems, the same sections can be read with the `man` command, and the master document is the one from `man perl`, which any Unix user would automatically use first to learn about perl.

Now you can browse each of the different listed sections simply by typing `perldoc` followed by the section name:

```
% perldoc perldelta
NAME
      perldelta - what's new for perl5.005

DESCRIPTION
      This document describes differences between the 5.004
      release and this one.
[...]
```

The list of sections you see under `perldoc perl` has thoughtfully been arranged in a logical order for browsing. Here are our quick tips that tell you which section to use for a particular purpose:

- **perlsyn:** Perl programs are made up largely of variables being manipulated by function calls or operators. What's in between the variables, functions, and operators is syntax. Here you'll find all the information on, for instance, how looping statements work, and how to put an `if` modifier after a statement.

- **perldata:** This section tells you about all the different kinds of variables you can create in your programs. Don't look here for multidimensional arrays (lists of lists, in Perl parlance) though; we'll get to them.

- **perlop:** Here you'll learn all about Perl's vast panoply of operators, ranging from the mundane + - * / to the magical powers of applying postincrement (++) to strings. There are some entries you might not expect to find here: the use of commas to separate list members, the different ways of quoting strings and how interpolation works inside them, how the `m//` (match) and `s///` (substitute) operators work (but the regular expressions they take as an argument are documented under **perlre**), the use of backticks to capture program output, reading lines from filehandles, and the mysteries of floating point numbers.

- **perlre:** This is where you can find out how to write regular expressions. Perl has easily the most powerful, "featureful" implementation of regular expressions anywhere. This section covers all the details from the most basic to the most advanced; read as far as you can without your head actually exploding and leave the rest for when you recover your strength.

- **perllol:** When you want to know how to implement multidimensional arrays, or complex data structures, this is the place to come. "lol" stands for "lists of lists," which strictly speaking is a misnomer since it really means "arrays or hashes of references to arrays or hashes," but is considerably more euphonious. If you've come from Pascal, Fortran, or C and are wondering where records or structs are, look no further. If you want to know all about how to make and use the references that enable lists of lists to be built, see **perlref**.

- **perlsub:** This contains everything you'd want to know about how to write your own subroutines (functions or procedures) in

Perl and far, far more, including entries you might not expect to find, on the `local` command and typeglobs. Pick the parts you need judiciously and save the eye-glazing sections for later.

We've left out many of the sections to avoid overwhelming you at this stage. Head back to `perldoc perl` when you feel up to it to see the more advanced ones we omitted.

One less advanced section we failed to list is `perlfunc`. The reason is that only rarely in your career will you want to peruse `perlfunc` in linear order.[8] That's because it consists of an alphabetical list of all Perl's myriad built-in functions, many of which you will never need. Fortunately, the `-f` option to `perldoc` allows you to name the function you're looking for:

```
% perldoc -f split
split /PATTERN/,EXPR,LIMIT
split /PATTERN/,EXPR
split /PATTERN/
split

Splits a string into an array of strings, and returns it.
By default, empty leading fields are preserved, and empty
trailing ones are deleted.
[...]
```

One last feature of `perldoc` is worth explaining. The Perl documentation goes to superhuman lengths to answer frequently asked questions, so much so that the FAQ comprises *nine* files. Simply scanning the FAQ for a particular topic (and don't assume your question isn't there—it covers some broad ground) is a daunting task. But the alternative is to risk being scorched by a cast of thousands if you post your question to the Net. So `perldoc` makes it a little easier for you to tell if your question is frequently asked with the `-q word` option,[9] which searches all the frequently asked questions (but not

---

8. That's an understatement. While understatement isn't a documented virtue of Perl programmers, it appears to be a virtue of Perl authors.

9. Actually, the argument can be a regular expression.

their answers) for word, and then shows you both the questions and their answers:

```
% perldoc -q sleep
Found in /usr/local/perl/lib/5.6.0/pod/perlfaq8.pod

How can I sleep() or alarm() for under a second?

If you want finer granularity than the 1 second that the sleep()
function provides, [...]
```

You can see more information about the Perl FAQ (and the FAQ itself) at `http://perlfaq.cpan.org/`.

`perldoc` can also display the source of a module with the -m option, which saves you the trouble of searching @INC for it.

But what if you're looking for something in the entire set of Perl documentation? Time to use the tools your computer comes with. To find the POD files that mention "readline,"

- On Unix (using csh or a variant):
  ```
  % find `perl -e '$_="@INC";s/ \.|\. //;print'` \
    -name "*.pod" -print | xargs grep -l readline
  /usr/local/perl/lib/5.00503/pod/perldebug.pod
  /usr/local/perl/lib/5.00503/pod/perlfaq5.pod
  /usr/local/perl/lib/5.00503/pod/perlfunc.pod
  /usr/local/perl/lib/5.00503/pod/perlmodlib.pod
  /usr/local/perl/lib/5.00503/pod/perlop.pod
  /usr/local/perl/lib/5.00503/pod/perltoc.pod
  /usr/local/perl/lib/5.00503/pod/perltrap.pod
  ```
  Explanation: We tell Perl to print the directories in which it searches for modules, remove the current directory from the list, then use the list as the argument to the find command to search for POD files whose names are printed by grep if they contain a match. These files should all be in the same directory, so once you know what it is, you can just grep in that directory and dis-

pense with the `find`. (But remember that `find` command if later on you want to search all the `.pm` files for something.) To get more relevant hits for common terms, pipe the results through another `grep` that searches for `=head`; then you'll find matches only in headings.

- On Windows:

  In ActiveState Perl, navigate to the HTML directory under the root of the installation and use Tools → Find in the Explorer to look for all files named `*.html` containing the text `readline`. If you have another build of Perl that didn't create HTML files from all the PODs, navigate to the root of the installation and find files named `*.pod`.

- On the Macintosh:

  Use `shuck`. (See the next section.)

1.5.3 Perl Documentation in MacPerl

The Perl port to the Macintosh by Matthias Neeracher includes a simple GUI utility application—shuck—to view POD files.[10] As shown in Figure 1-1, shuck reads a POD file, then renders a properly formatted version of the file in a standard Mac floating window.

1.6 References

Learn the ins and outs of Perl programming from (in rough order of importance):

- *Programming Perl,* 3rd ed., by Larry Wall, Tom Christiansen and Jon Orwant (O'Reilly & Associates, 2000)

---

10. Again, refer to the **Getting Perl** section in the Preface for instructions on how to obtain MacPerl.

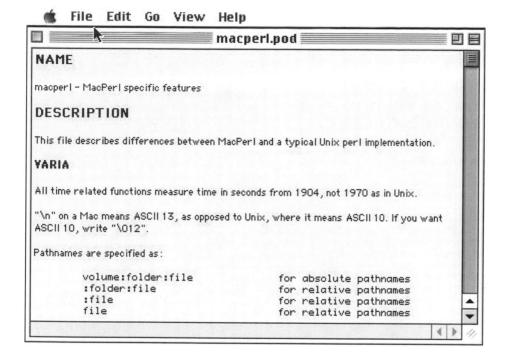

FIGURE 1-1. The `macperl` POD file viewed in shuck

- *Object Oriented Perl,* by Damian Conway (Manning Publications, 1999).

- *Effective Perl Programming,* by Joseph Hall with Randal Schwartz (Addison-Wesley, 1998).

- *The Perl Cookbook,* by Tom Christiansen and Nathan Torkington (O'Reilly & Associates, 1998).

- *Mastering Regular Expressions,* by Jeffrey Friedl (O'Reilly & Associates, 1997).

- *Perl 5 Pocket Reference,* 3rd ed., by Johan Vromans (O'Reilly & Associates, 2000).

- `http://search.cpan.org/` Access to finding modules in the Comprehensive Perl Archive Network.
- `http://www.perldoc.com/` Access to the standard documentation and much more.

## Chapter 2

The Zen of Perl Developing

"Wild nights are my glory."

Mrs. Whatsit in A Wrinkle in Time, *by Madeleine L'Engle*

We've come to realize there are two sides to programming: the left-brain, formal minutiae of creating smart code; and the right-brain, soft, touchy-feely stuff that goes on in your head.

Most programmers would rather ignore the touchy-feely stuff because it's just Not Their Thing. However, we've found that it's more important than the rational left-brain information, because it affects everything you do. So we're going to cover the soft stuff first, because it's what happens first in your head. This leads us to a touchy-feely Perl of Wisdom:

 First know yourself; then your programs will be easier to know.

Go out and about among programmers, and soon you discover some are better than others—a lot better. It has been a source of fascination to us as to why there is such variation in performance—we're talking about orders of magnitude differences in speed, accuracy, and maintainability between the best and the worst for any given task—and we've come to learn that most of that difference is due to *attitudes, beliefs,* and *behaviors* that set them apart from the rest.

Yes, talent and innate intelligence count for a lot, but less than you might think. Yes, knowledge and experience are required for creating quality programs, but they can be enervated by poor attitudes and limiting beliefs.

 This isn't just psychobabble; I see it all the time in my classes. It's common to see people with a problem freeze at the keyboard, unable to take any action. They're afraid that if they experiment, they'll break something. They're suffering from a limiting belief that the computer is more fragile than it really is.

This is good news! Because wise people know that they can change their attitudes, beliefs, and behaviors, and know how.

Where does Perl fit in here? Perl is designed to put your convenience above abstract notions of aesthetics or elegance. Perl is designed to make it as easy as possible for you to go from an idea for solving a problem to creating the solution itself, no matter what computing background you hail from. There are so many Ways To Do It in Perl because Perl is a polyglot. Other computer languages are like your eighth-grade French teacher:

> You: "Miss, miss, there's a fire in the stockroom!"

> Them: "Ah-ah-ah-ah! Et, maintenant *en Français*, s'il vous plaît!"

Whereas Perl will go out of its way to understand you:

> You: "Yo, fraulein mine, yon edifice hast une conflagation, eh wot?"

> Perl: "Sounds like you're saying there's a fire over there...I'll get help!"

Let's look at which attitudes, beliefs, and behaviors best serve us.

2.1 Attitudes

You don't just have relationships with people (although some people spend so long at their keyboards that we might wonder whether they have even those); you have relationships with everything you interact with, and that includes your computer and your programs. And if you don't think you have a relationship, or don't believe you have a relationship with them, then you have the unconscious "this-isn't-a-relationship" relationship.

This isn't just New Age hocus-pocus; this is at the core of how successful you are when you get behind a keyboard. What's your first reaction when you do that? Somewhere on a scale between "Oh boy—I can't believe I get paid for this!" and "Rats. Work again. Can't wait for the ball game on Saturday."

This isn't just measuring your reaction, it's measuring your enthusiasm; and your enthusiasm is directly related to how well you do.

Sometimes enthusiasm is caused by fear, instead of passion—when your boss tells you to finish a project by tomorrow or you're fired, you wouldn't call your resulting emotional state *enthusiastic*, but you would call it *motivated*. This is nearly as effective as enthusiasm deriving from passion, but it's a poor substitute—the resulting stress, anger, and resentment will take their toll. So here's our first Perl of Wisdom on enthusiasm:

④ Motivate yourself by what you want to move *toward*, not what you want to *get away from*.

In this line of business you are generally in enough demand that you don't have to continue working for a boss who uses threats to motivate you; but if it happens anyway, don't bring that anger and fear to the keyboard (because it's harder to think clearly through those emotions). Think instead of what it is that your job brings you that makes keeping it a good thing: the health plan that keeps your family well, the money that keeps you fed and clothed, the opportunity to create beautiful things. There. Don't you feel better when you look at it that way?

Perl has some commentary about attitudes as well. (The Perl documentation waxes quite philosophical, theosophical, and ontological at times.) It tells us that the three principal virtues of a programmer are laziness, hubris, and impatience. Why?

- Laziness: Because doing the same thing more than once is the sign of bad code design. If you're naturally lazy, you'll naturally balk at the idea of repeating yourself.
- Hubris: A fancy word for egotistical pride. Let's face it; you need *chutzpah* to be a programmer. Just to think that you can outwit

something whose innards nobody knows *in toto,* that you can defeat the bugs known and unknown, takes confidence bordering on recklessness. The main reason that so many people do it is for the ego boost from creating something that others will associate with them. (This is not to denigrate the well thought out concept of "egoless programming" promulgated by Gerald Weinberg... but you'll notice it hasn't exactly caught on everywhere either. Programmers tend to be more hubristic than most.)

- Impatience: Because you're not doing this just for the sake of typing at a keyboard; you want to create something. Perl was created to satisfy the thousands of people who had grown tired of spending so much of their development time satisfying the demands of their language rather than the requirements of their solution. So turn on that impatience filter, and start noticing when you're doing things that you shouldn't have to. If you can see how a machine could be doing something you're doing, get the machine to do it if it saves time in the long run. Life's too short to waste on pointless typing.

2.2 Beliefs

By *beliefs,* we mean those silly little thoughts that we hold unspoken inside, which would, if exposed to the light of rationalism, fall apart in a second's worth of examination. Like the belief that makes you kick the lawn mower when it doesn't start even though the only outcome is to stub your toe ("This thing should work and I'm punishing it for misbehaving"). Or the belief that makes you snap at your spouse for not putting the cap on the toothpaste tube even though you make as many mistakes of that nature as he/she does ("They should live up to certain standards which I punish even myself for not meeting"). Or, to use a more familiar example, the belief that error return checking can be omitted ("It's only a little test program...nothing will go wrong").

Beliefs can be either enabling ("I can do this!") or limiting. Check out these common limiting beliefs and see if anything sounds familiar:

  • "I could never be as good a programmer as so-and-so."

  • "My programs just never work right."

  • "I could never understand that complicated computer science stuff."

How good a person you believe yourself to be is termed *self-esteem*. And yes, it does have a bearing on how well you program. It's been our experience that the people with low self-esteem (insufficient hubris, in Perl terminology) are the ones who unconsciously compare themselves to the computer and come up short. If you think the computer's going to beat you, you've handicapped yourself unnecessarily. You need the gall to believe that you can handle any problem it can hurl your way. Even the kind you've never met before. Of course, nothing feeds the ego like a track record of success, but some people who have that track record still don't acknowledge it. And if you don't have that track record yet, how can you get it? What resources do you have for improving your knowledge, skill, and experience?

To sit in front of a computer with a limiting belief is to handicap yourself before you even begin. But it's not always easy to tell that you have limiting beliefs, because they almost always go unspoken, unvoiced even in your thoughts. They just sit there like a faceless bureaucrat in an anonymous government office rubberstamping "Application Denied" on your hopes and ambitions.

So, like an astronomer finding a black hole, you identify a limiting belief by its effect on what surrounds it. A good way to do this is by observing changes in your mood that have no good explanation. If you're working on a program and realize that while you entered the office in an upbeat mood, you're now sitting under a cloud of funk, ask yourself what changed, and when? If you're aware enough to notice that it happened the moment you sat in front of the keyboard, what was going through your mind at the time?

Like firefly flashes in the night, limiting beliefs trigger sudden negative statements that zip through your brain almost too quickly to notice. Was it the "Computers always end up beating me" thought? Or the "I'm afraid I'll screw something up horribly" thought? Or one of thousands of other possibilities? Whatever it was, the moment you catch it, it will dissolve under the power of awareness like blowing on a dandelion. Because you know that whatever your history, you're not bound to repeat it, and you know if you talk with the right people about what you're doing, no honest mistake is going to be catastrophic.

2.3 Behavior

Talking about resources for improving your expertise leads us to our last touchy-feely concept: behaviors. If you have the right attitude and a good set of beliefs, you need to follow up with right behaviors, or, if you prefer, "good habits." Check these out.

2.3.1 Neatness

Sloppy organization leads to a sloppy mindset, which leads to sloppy code. Never mind how tidy your office is; do you have a bunch of files called `foo`, `tmp`, `fred`, `latest`, `latest2`, and so on lying around? Get rid of them or archive them somewhere with meaningful labels. Do you follow a consistent indentation style? If not, copy the style of a good programmer whose code you like until you feel like tweaking it for personal taste. Just be consistent!

2.3.2 Communication

How sure are you of the requirements for the program you're writing? Have you checked with the customer what they mean by the various terms they used? Have you explained to them what assumptions you made in interpreting their requirements?

2.3.3 Experimentation

Time and time again, people ask, "What would happen if I did X?" when they could actually try it in less time than it would take to get the answer (which might be wrong). Don't spend ages trying to second-guess the machine; find out. If there were a fourth virtue in the Perl canon, it would be *curiosity*. If you're not eager to find out what would happen in some odd situation cooked up by your fertile mind, then cultivate the attitude of curiosity, because people who have it will move along the learning curve much faster than those who don't.

The way to feel comfortable experimenting is to know your boundaries. Many people are afraid of breaking the machine or destroying data. So learn which sorts of actions could do that, and which are safe. Find the safest playground you can. If you have a PC with some spare disk space, you can create extra partitions just for a special version of your favorite operating system if you're afraid of hurting something important. A tool like Partition Magic will make this process easy. Then take something that works, and intentionally break it. Explore all the ways it can go wrong. If you've created a "throwaway" Linux on its own partitions, find out just how hard it is to damage it. After enough of this kind of play, you'll have a good idea of what you can get away with and be much less anxious when you're debugging in a real environment.

Curiosity is an essential quality of the people who develop Perl and who spend inordinate amounts of time trying out the strangest pieces of code you've ever seen, all in an attempt to explore the boundaries of Perl, and maybe to break it.

2.3.4 Precision

Perl works hard to accommodate different ways of thinking and different styles of programming. This *laissez faire* acceptance does not mean there aren't rigorous definitions of the terminology of Perl itself, though. To communicate accurately with others and keep things straight in your own mind, learn the proper terms for everything you use and be ruthless about keeping them straight. For instance, there is a huge difference between lists and arrays in Perl: make sure you know what it is.[1] When you say "system call," do you

---

1. See "What is the difference between a list and an array?" in `perlfaq4`.

mean a call that uses the operating system or a `system()` call? When you say "local variables," are you referring to private variables declared with `my` or temporary copies of package variables declared with `our` or `local`?

2.4 *Improve Your Craft*

If you love what you're doing, improving your skills comes naturally. If you don't, doing it better is an uphill battle. (Do you really need to do it if you don't like it?) The avenues for getting better at what you do are numerous. Any time you feel that you've conquered the mountain, you might check out the Software Engineering Institute's Capability Maturity Model for software development (SW-CMM),[2] which delineates five levels that development groups may achieve in order of increasing effectiveness. Few groups have ever been certified at level 5. Something to aim for.

2.5 *The Bottom Line*

If you've got good attitudes and beliefs, the right behaviors are easy to learn—they're mostly details. So in the next chapter, we'll get back to the left-brain mode of programming details and discuss useful behaviors.

---

2. `http://www.sei.cmu.edu/cmm/cmm.html`

Chapter 3

Antibugging

"It is a capital mistake to theorize before one has data.

Insensibly one begins to twist facts to suit theories

instead of theories to suit facts."

Sherlock Holmes in A Scandal in Bohemia, *by Sir Arthur Conan Doyle*

As you can tell from the chapter title, we're not above coining horrible neologisms to save space. (When our publisher pays us by the word, we'll be happy to be more verbose, but paying us by the word would be as sensible as measuring programmers' performance by how many lines of code they write.)

Antibugging describes a set of programming techniques that minimize the probability of introducing a bug to a program at design time or input. You could also call it *defensive programming*. We're applying the principles we developed in the previous chapter to come up with some good Perl development behaviors.

3.1 Beginning

Before you turn your ideas into code, describe them in natural language.

 If you can't say it in natural language, you won't be able to say it in Perl.

The Extreme Programming methodology (mentioned in more detail in Chapter 6) is helpful in this respect in that by insisting that tests be written before the code they test, and requiring programming in pairs, it encourages this kind of conversation.

 I've seen this too many times: someone is having horrible difficulties doing an exercise and the code is bleeding all over the screen. Yet when I ask them to describe how it's supposed to work, they can't articulate it. This is a large clue that the approach wasn't completely thought out to begin with.

3.2 *Writing Code*

Your code should be as pleasing to the eye as possible, if for no other reason than you should like looking at it and not recoil at the prospect of again diving into an eructation of characters on the screen. And let's face it, programs need all the aesthetic help they can get because their primary purpose is utilitarian. Which of the following subroutines do you prefer?

```
sub iterate (&$$){
for ($_[1] = 0,my $i = 0;$i <= $_[2];
$_[1] = ++$i/$_[2]){&{$_[0] };
}
}
```

or

```
sub iterate (&$$)
   {
   for ($_[1] = 0, my $i = 0;
       $i <= $_[2];
       $_[1] = ++$i / $_[2])
     {
     &{$_[0]};
     }
   }
```

3.2.1 Style

The only believable comment to make about style is that you should have one. If you aren't already rabidly attached to a particular style, read the `perlstyle` manual page and adopt the one shown.

There's no excuse for not indenting properly. I have seen many people in my classes struggling with an exercise, needlessly handicapped because their code was all hugging the left margin for grim death. Regardless of how quick, short, or temporary your code is, indenting it will save more time than it costs. (The Emacs `cperl` mode will autoindent simply by hitting the `TAB` key.)

 6   **Use a consistent style for each project.**

 A clean style is a good style, whatever style you choose. A suggestion: write your code as though you expect it to be published (and win the Turing Award)—using white space galore and ample comments.

Pick clear variable names. In general, the less often a variable appears in your code (or the smaller its scope), the longer its name should be since the reader will need more reminding of its purpose. There's nothing wrong though, with single-letter variable names for loop variables (for which they have a long and distinguished history) or mathematical or scientific quantities. (`$e=$m*$c**2` makes just as much sense as `$energy=$mass*$speed_of_light**2`, at least it does to anyone who should be using code that computes it.)

3.2.2 Help from Your Editor

For those of you concerned about going blind counting and matching `()`, `{}`, and `[]` symbols in your programs, there are tools that can save you from the white cane. A smart editor that can help with some of the routine chores of beautifying a Perl program works wonders. If you have to reindent your code manually every time you remove an outer block, chances are you won't do it. Perl gurus are fond of stating, "Only perl can parse Perl," and as a corollary, no editor can be smart enough to lay out all possible Perl programs correctly. Fair enough; but some of them come close enough to be useful.

One of Peter's favorites is `cperl`, a Perl mode for Emacs maintained by Ilya Zakharevich. The standard Perl distribution includes an `emacs` directory that contains the file `cperl-mode.el`. If your Emacs doesn't already come with `cperl`, copy this file to wherever you store local Emacs mode files (you can set up a location just for yourself in the `.emacs` file in your home directory); if you find another version there, determine which `cperl-mode.el` is more recent. Insert the line

```
(autoload 'perl-mode "cperl-mode" "alternate mode for editing \
Perl programs" t)
```

into your `.emacs` file to enable `cperl-mode` instead of the regular `perl-mode` that comes with Emacs.

`cperl` matches up the various `()`, `[]`, and `{}` for you.[1] It also performs syntax coloring, so if you configure Emacs to tint all strings in puce and your entire file suddenly blushes, you know you've left a quote mark out somewhere. Most usefully, it tracks nested levels of braces, and a tap of the `TAB` key takes you to the correct indentation point for the line. This catches all manner of typos, such as the dropped semicolon on line 1:

```
1  my $marsupial = 'wombat'
2      my $crustacean = 'king crab';
```

which is exposed when you hit `TAB` on line 2 and instead of lining up under line 1, the statement indents an extra level because the current statement is incomplete.

`cperl` does have a few problems, though: if you use the Perl 4 syntax for separating path components in a package qualified identifier with a single quote, it may get confused. But just change the apostrophe (`'`) to colons (`::`), and you're fine. Using certain characters (like `#` or `'`) in character classes in regular expressions confuses it too, but putting backslashes (`\`) in front of them (*backwhacking*) resolves the problem.

---

1. ... among other things; it also allows Emacs to function as a front end to the perl debugger. Debugging with Emacs is discussed in Chapter 7.

Other editors we like are: vim/gvim, which does an outstanding job of syntax coloring and has an excellent Windows port; and BBEdit on the Macintosh.

The subject of favorite editors is an intensely religious issue in software development, and you should expect others to disagree with your preference; as long as there are some equally heavyweight developers on your side, it doesn't matter what you pick or what anyone else says.

What should you expect from a good Perl editor? It should warn you when you have mismatched delimiters, it should automatically indent according to the style you want, and it should be as flexible and adaptable to your personal text-editing needs as possible. It should neither insert characters (e.g., invisible binary formatting hints) nor remove any (e.g., trailing spaces) on its own without warning you and giving you the option to disable this functionality selectively or globally.

3.2.3 Think Double

Whether your editor warns you of mismatched delimiters or not, here's a handy tip: enter the closing delimiter at the same time you type the opening one. Then insert what you need between them. Work from the outside in, and your chances of having a grouping typo are greatly reduced. For instance, if you plan to write something that'll end up as:

```
print table(map { Tr(map td($_), split /[:\s]+/) } <IN>);
```

(which, using `CGI.pm`, would print an HTML table from the remaining text coming from the filehandle `IN`, one row per line, forming table elements from elements separated by white space and/or colons) then your strategy for typing it would follow these steps:

```
1.   print table();
2.   print table(map {} <>);
3.   print table(map { Tr() } <IN>);
4.   print table(map { Tr(map td(), split //) } <IN>);
5.   print table(map { Tr(map td($_), split /[:\s]+/) } <IN>);
```

3.2.4 Clarity

Examine this very simple one-line program:

```
$x=1; $y=2; $z=$x+$y; print"$x+$y=$z\n";
```

This isn't difficult to understand: initialize $x and $y, set $z to their sum, then print all three. Suppose we trace its execution through the debugger (see Chapter 7 for a detailed discussion of the debugger).

```
perl -de '$x=1; $y=2; $z=$x+$y; print"$x+$y=$z\n"'
main::(-e:1):$x=1; $y=2; $z=$x+$y; print"$x+$y=$z\n";
  DB<1> n
main::(-e:1):$x=1; $y=2; $z=$x+$y; print"$x+$y=$z\n"
  DB<1> n
main::(-e:1):$x=1; $y=2; $z=$x+$y; print"$x+$y=$z\n"
  DB<1> n
main::(-e:1):$x=1; $y=2; $z=$x+$y; print"$x+$y=$z\n"
  DB<1> n
1+2=3
Debugged program terminated...
  DB<1> q
```

What did we observe? The debugger prints the one-line program:

```
main::(-e:1):$x=1; $y=2; $z=$x+$y; print"$x+$y=$z\n"
```

4 times until the expected program output 1+2=3. Why? The debugger displays the next line of code perl executes, not the next command. The program consists of four executable commands, but they're all on the same line; therefore we see the line each time the debugger executes a commend.

Recast the program to one command per line:

```
$x = 1;
$y = 2;
$z = $x+$y;
print"$x+$y=$z\n";
```

Then use the debugger. You can either put the four lines in a file or use a shell like the Bourne shell that allows you to type new lines between single quotes.

```
perl -d dbformat.pl
main::(dbformat.pl:1):$x=1;
  DB<1> n
main::(dbformat.pl:2):$y=2;
  DB<1> n
main::(dbformat.pl:3):$z=$x+$y;
  DB<1> n
main::(dbformat.pl:4):print"$x+$y=$z\n";
  DB<1> n
1+2=3
Debugged program terminated...
  DB<1> q
```

This is easier to follow. The debugger functioned as it was designed to in both cases, but a style difference made it harder to interpret the debugger's output for the one-liner.

3.3 Observation

One of the most important skills you can hone as a developer is the power of observation. The biggest lesson to learn is how *not* to make things up. One way to learn this is to spend a stint answering calls on a help desk. Because so many of the people who call give such blatantly incomplete, inaccurate, or imaginary information, you will quickly realize the proper ways to describe a problem.

Why is this important to you as a developer? It's about better communication, and better understanding. *Better communication* because when you're working with someone else, you have to convey your ideas and experiences to them in the slow, limited medium of speech rather than in the lightning fast way in which richly expressive thoughts zip around in your head. Until development teams can use mind melds to communicate, you have to make the best of the bandwidth bottleneck called your tongue. *Better understanding* because whenever you articulate something inaccurately, even if you're the only one listening, part of you will take it at face value and then get confused.

How does this "making things up" show up? Let's say someone is running a program containing the following code for sending a report back to them:

```
open MAIL, "|$SENDMAIL $address"
  and print MAIL "Subject: Report for ". localtime, "\n\n"
  and print MAIL `/usr/local/bin/dbquery $month $day`
  and close MAIL
  or die "Unable to send to $address: $!\n";
```

But on execution they receive an empty e-mail message. On further inspection, they see the program (let's call it `frozzle`) had printed:

```
Can't exec "/usr/local/bin/dbquery": Permission denied at ...
```

At this point, they contact their system administrator and say, "Hey, the `frozzle` program doesn't have permission to deliver mail to me."

What happens? The sysadmin goes off on a wild goose chase for misset mailbox permissions, wrong firewall settings, or broken `sendmail` rules.

Well, usually not. Any sysadmin worth his or her salt will not take this problem report at face value but instead will ask these three questions:

- What did you do?
- How did the computer react?
- What were you expecting it to do instead?

And the answers to these questions require *absolutely no computer knowledge, intelligence, or guesswork whatsoever,* just observation:

- I ran the `frozzle` program.
- It printed `Can't exec "/usr/local/bin/dbquery"` ... and I received a blank e-mail message.
- Usually it prints nothing, and I get a report in my e-mail.

However, today it is common for administrative layers to interpose themselves between the user and their system administrator. If the user has to call a help desk that transcribes their problem report into a trouble ticket database, then assigns a sysadmin from a pool to work on the problem, the chances are much higher the sysadmin will end up on a wild goose chase (particularly since the help desk probably assigned the ticket to the mail server group).

When you're dealing with customers, you'll train them to describe their problems in terms of answering the three questions. But even as a developer, you'll need to be adept at doing so yourself. When something goes wrong, know the difference between what happened and your guesses at what it means. As developers, we've often gone on goose chases much wilder than the one described earlier, all because we got some bee in our bonnet about what we thought was really happening.

3.4 Documentation

We know, real programmers don't document. "It was hard to write; it should be hard to understand." We feel your pain. However, the sanity you save may be your own. You could hop between jobs sufficiently rapidly that you never have to revisit a program you wrote more than six months ago.[2] Or you could document it so you'll understand what you did.

Reams of valuable material have been written on the subject of program documentation, most of it by people who aren't programmers or who would be considered fringe programmers at best by people who think of themselves as "real" programmers. If documentation is your nemesis, we don't intend to try and emulate the worthy people who can tell you exactly how and why you should write scads of hierarchical documents.

Because we hate it too.

---

2. But if you never write programs for your personal use, you can't consider yourself a *true* programmer.

So here, instead, is the lazy person's guide to documentation, based purely upon selfish motives. (Of course, in some programming environments, you have no choice but to write copious documentation, because management requires it. These environments are rare, in our experience.)

1. Imagine this is a program written by someone else, and you've been asked or ordered to take it over. What help do you need to understand it? As crazy as this scenario sounds, it's as close to the truth as anything else. Many times, you *will* have to do something with a program you wrote but haven't seen for more than six months, and many times, you won't remember nearly enough about how you wrote it to get back up to speed.

2. If it was quick to write and easy to understand, don't waste time documenting it. There *is* such a thing as self-documenting code, and the better you are at writing it, the less time you'll have to waste explaining yourself. Not all code is self-documenting, of course. Nevertheless, writing the following calls for some comment and scrutiny:

```
for (my $i = 0; $i <= $#a; $i++)
  {
  $b[$i] = $a[$i] * 86400;
  }
```

Whereas in writing

```
@seconds = map $_ * $SECS_PER_DAY, @days
```

it probably wouldn't.

3. The parts you *do* need to document are those that took you a long time to figure out. The amount of commenting accompanying any given piece of code should be proportional to the time it took to create it.

I once spent about a month getting *one number* right in a program. It was a driver for a communications board, and the number represented the combined flag settings for a rather important register. The vendor documentation was inadequate for divining the correct settings, and each attempt at ringing the combinations required many hours of exhaustive regression testing. That one number received a *lot* of commenting when we got it right.

4. It's not enough to say *how* things work, you also have to say *why*. Any time you make a choice that isn't obvious, explain it. Otherwise when you come back to it in six months, you'll be staring at that spot wondering, "Why did I do it that way? There's a much more obvious way…"

5. Comments are not enough. They may explain the how and the why of the code, but they don't say why you were doing it in the first place. Whether or not you put it in the same file as the code, somewhere you need a user guide for the person using your code, and you also need to capture the thoughts that went into the code's design. Why is there a module at this point in your class hierarchy? If you read your data from a flat file, instead of an Oracle database that everyone else uses, because your data file contains one more attribute than the database captures, say so. If it took thought to come up with, the thought needs to be captured somewhere.

Perl provides a couple of ways of documenting as you code, and in the ideal place for documentation—right next to the code itself.[3] The first way is the old dependable comment-to-end-of-line, used for informing a code maintainer of the operation of tricky code or why certain nonobvious choices were made. The second way is POD—plain old documentation—a rudimentary system of

---

3. Brad Appleton terms the reason that this is advantageous the *locality principle of reference documentation* and has an extensive discussion on it at `http://c2.com/cgi/wiki? LocalityOfReferenceDocumentation`.

embedding interface documentation in the program itself, which can later be extracted into Unix man pages, HTML, or other formats by programs included with perl.[4]

 ## 7   Comment the hard parts. Use POD.

This documentation is for the user of the program or module, someone who might be lucky enough never to need to look at your actual code. The advantage of putting this documentation in the same file as the code is twofold: it reduces the number of files you need to ship, and it enables you to put external documentation as close as you like to the actual code it refers to. (Although not out of sequence—POD is like a gap-toothed backwoods cousin of WEB, Donald Knuth's "literate programming" tool which was flexible enough to do that reordering and capable of producing wonderfully typeset annotated versions of your program. Unfortunately, the WEB user also had to learn T_EX and learn how to embed T_EX and program code in a hieroglyphic soup that made TECO macros read like Dr. Seuss. But enough nostalgia.)

POD is almost certainly the best choice for your user documentation, because people expect to find it in Perl files.

 To be blunt, a proper program is defined by the set consisting of the executable code, comments that describe the how and why of the code, and documentation describing the function of the program (with examples). Real men and women comment their code!

---

4. Look for the programs pod2man, pod2html, or pod2anything-else-you-might-want-to-use.

3.5 Developing

There's no substitute for knowledge. Coding something you don't understand should set off warning bells in your brain: "What does the code I just wrote really do?" That's the time to experiment.

 I have seen too many people take a shotgun approach to coding: they just fire a blast of characters onto the screen and rearrange them until something works. Too often, instructors foster the mindset that the only thing that counts is getting the right answer: I keep finding people who put something in a program "because it works"—in *that* particular situation—but don't understand what they are doing and so can't extend it to other situations or aren't aware of how it might fail.

Nevertheless, there are times when you have to do something quite beyond your current ability or the rate at which you can learn something new. Here are some useful ways to cheat:

1. **Steal.** Tom Christiansen and Nathan Torkington have gone and left a pile of code in a fat book[5] at your local bookstore which you can use for anything you want and they'll never complain. If you find the task you're trying to solve in there, have at it. You can always break your overall task into smaller logical units that are more generic and therefore more likely to be in the book.

2. **Mutate.** Start by using good code that does something similar to what you want, and gradually change it to fit your needs. Even though there may be code you don't understand in there, it may stay isolated from your changes, so you don't have to worry about it. (Anyone who has subclassed a module is familiar with

---

5. *The Perl Cookbook* (O'Reilly & Associates, 1998).

this way of thinking.) How do you recognize good code? Emulate the best.

Now, whenever we've asked who to emulate, people have been reluctant to name anyone in particular. We applaud their sense of fairness but the result is frustrating. Therefore we present our totally biased, incomplete, but still useful list of authors whose code you can find on the net, the copying of which will likely lead to good results.[6] We've put the names in alphabetical order to avoid any more outrage than necessary.

Gisle Aas	Uri Guttman	Chip Salzenberg
Greg Bacon	Joseph N. Hall	Gurusamy Sarathy
Graham Barr	Jarkko Hietaniemi	Randal Schwartz
Tim Bunce	Nick Ing-Simmons	Michael G. Schwern
Alan Burlison	Ronald Kimball	Lincoln Stein
Nigel Chapman	John Macdonald	Mike Stok
Tom Christiansen	Tad McClellan	Nathan Torkington
Damian Conway	Chris Nandor	Hugo van der Sanden
Simon Cozens	Jon Orwant	Johan Vromans
Mark-Jason Dominus	Tom Phoenix	Larry Wall
Jan Dubois	John Porter	Ilya Zakharevich
`brian d foy`	Larry Rosler	

Note to the obviousness-challenged: this wasn't a popularity contest and we're not handing out awards. Of course there are dozens of other people we could have added, and hundreds more are worthy of inclusion in such a list if only we were aware of them all. (And if you're in that category, we apologize

---

6. However, if you see any code posted by these or other people with references to either golf or bowling, it means they're competing to see who can solve the problem in either the smallest or largest number of characters. The winner in either case is unlikely to be highly comprehensible. See `http:/` `/www.perlfaq.com/faqs/id/154`.

to you.) We print it here because it's the kind of list we wanted, and couldn't find, when we were beginning Perl. Arbitrary and incomplete as it is, we believe it to be superior to no list at all.

Now, when you're mutating code, be sure and test that the original works before you change it![7] This admonition has nothing to do with the reliability of its author, rather the fact that everyone's environment is different, and maybe the difference between yours and the author's is significant. (Sometimes we have spent ages trying to find bugs in changes we made while mutating code only to find that the problem was in the original.)

Then modify as little at a time as possible to get something you can test. Change the parts you understand the best first—like the names of input/output files and e-mail logging addresses—test, and keep going with the harder parts. With luck, you'll eventually end up with what you need without having to touch the parts you don't understand. (Anyone who's subclassed a module and had to override the constructor and other methods is familiar with this approach.)

3.6 Accident Prevention

These tips fall into the category of installing sprinklers instead of polishing your fire hose.

3.6.1 Be Strict

Put the directive `use strict` as the first line (after the `#!` line if there is one) of every file (including modules you write; strictness is lexically scoped, not program scoped). Especially if you don't understand why. This makes Perl, well, stricter about things that you could get away with without it that are nevertheless usually mistakes. It is telling that the one group of people whose expertise would most allow them to get away without using `strict` (the

---

7. This and some of our other tips fall under the category Joseph N. Hall termed "Don't overlook the obvious" in *Effective Perl Programming* (Addison-Wesley, 1998).

uppermost echelon of Perl experts) is the most adamant about its indispensabil-ity.[8]

Don't think it's faster to get your program working, then go back and insert the use strict, and clean up the resulting errors. It's much slower, for two reasons: first, developing without strictness results in errors being harder to find and taking longer to fix. Second, when you add strictness to a lengthy program that has never been strict before, the number of errors printed is likely to be enormous, and fixing them will probably not be trivial.

This is not an exaggeration, particularly if your nonstrict code has graduated to an operational environment. You may not have the option to shut things down while you recode and retest.

What makes use strict our friend is that most of the objections it raises prevent a program that is not following good practices from ever running. (This is called *raising a compile-time exception*. Although there is one class of errors it catches only at run-time.)

The biggest favor use strict does for you is to force you to declare all your variables with a my statement, or it will complain that you've referenced a variable without an explicit package name. In other words, variables not declared with my belong to a family of variables you seldom need to use; so seldom, in fact, that use strict requires you refer to such variables by their full names, which include the packages they live in.

Why is this such a huge favor? Because it guards against the ravages of the common typo. Consider this code:

```
my $enrolled_so_far = 0;
foreach my $student (@students)
    {
```

---

8. Except when they're entering the Obfuscated Perl Contest (www.tpj.com/contest), which relies heavily upon not using strict. That ought to tell you something.

```
    foreach my $class (keys %registry)
       {
       $enroled_so_far++, last
          if exists $registry{$class}{$student};
       }
    }
print "Number of enrollees so far = $enrolled_so_far\n";
```

Without use strict, this happily runs, producing the answer "0" no matter what the data. Because of the tiny typo in the innermost loop, perl increments a *different* variable called $enroled_so_far, which it automatically creates in this different family of variables we've been talking about. But under use strict, perl will refuse to run this code since $enroled_so_far has neither been introduced with a my statement nor is it qualified with a package name.[9]

Using use strict insulates you against a host of errors and parts of Perl that you may never need to learn.

8 Declare as many of your variables as possible to be lexical.

Many snippets of code in documentation or articles don't declare their variables with my; the authors consider it too encumbering for their examples. The code may work fine without use strict, but each variable is created automatically as a *dynamic* or *package* variable, which has slightly different behavior from a lexical variable and for which temporary versions are created using the old local keyword.

use strict forces you to distinguish between lexical variables and dynamic variables. There is very little reason to use the latter, or local, any more in Perl programs, with the exception of

   • Special per-package variables like @ISA

---

9. Perl being Perl, there are always exceptions (except when there aren't), and you can prevent perl from complaining about unqualified package variables with the our or use vars pragmas.

- Localizing special variables like $_ that can't be made lexical
- Package variables that you create and want to access from other classes for inheritance purposes

You will usually know what to do when you encounter one of these situations.

3.6.2 Let Yourself Off with a Warning

Always run your programs with the -w option to enable warnings. Some of these warnings come at compile time (for instance, declaring a my variable already declared in the same scope—you might think this would be reason enough to fail use strict, but Perl is curiously benevolent in this respect), and some of them come at run time because they can't be detected any earlier. (For instance, a warning that you used the value of an uninitialized variable or in some other way acquired the sentinel value undef.[10] Perl happily assigns a default value of 0 in numeric context and " " in string context to this variable, but chances are, it's a mistake for you to be reading an undefined variable at that point.)[11]

Now, opinion is somewhat divided on the matter of leaving the -w flag on in operational, or delivered, code. The ayes contend that since you designed your program not to generate any warnings under -w (referred to as "-w clean"), if it ever does so, that is an error, and it ought to be visible as such. The nays retort that even if you've eliminated these possibilities, one day new warnings that your program triggers may get added to Perl, and you wouldn't want your customers' delicate sensibilities offended by Perl's sometimes off-the-wall remarks. Besides, sometimes the warnings can go to an output filter of some kind (like a Web server—we'll show how to work with errors in CGI programs in Chapter 13) and confuse it.

---

10. Another exception: the warning doesn't occur if the operation you're performing on the undefined variable is ++. If you look at some code that uses ++ like that, you'll see why this is useful.

11. If you have a variable that could legitimately acquire a value of undef by that point in your program, then test for it using the defined operator.

We squirm on the fence and eventually fall down on the side of the ayes. The best-written code can go wrong in ways we never anticipated,[12] and the best tools are those that trap all kinds of errors and package them up for the maintainers like a drawstring cat litter box liner. Find ways of redirecting warnings in production code so that the information is saved but not necessarily exposed to the user, because if something that you're doing today generates a warning in a later version of Perl, it may cause a failure in the version of Perl that follows.

Perl 5.6.0 added a feature that greatly extended the `-w` functionality: lexical warnings. `perldoc perllexwarn` tells you how you can insert variants of the `use warnings` pragma to selectively enable and disable classes of warning in lexical scopes. Because the capability does not work with versions older than 5.6.0, and this book is not concerned with fine control over warnings, we stick to the `-w` syntax.

9   **Use -w and use strict in all your programs.**

Sometimes the one-liners perl spits out courtesy of `-w` are too succinct to figure out at first glance. You can find a longer explanation of the message by looking it up in the `perldiag` manual page, or you can insert the line `use diagnostics;` in your program, which causes the longer explanation to print along with the one-liner.

10   **Use use diagnostics to explain error messages.**

An alternative to changing your program or browsing through `perldiag` is to use the `splain` program distributed with perl. Just filter your program's output through `splain`, and it appends the longer explanation to each error message as though you'd used `diagnostics` in the first place.

---

12. *Peter*: I once wrote a program that ran in a 24/7 real-time environment successfully for nine *years* before a bug was encountered.

3.7 Tips for Reducing Complexity

"Complexity is the enemy, and our aim is to kill it."

Jan Baan

One of Perl's greatest strengths is its expressiveness and extreme conciseness. Complexity is the bane of software development: when a program grows beyond a certain size, it becomes much harder to test, maintain, read, or extend. Unfortunately, today's problems mean this is true for every program we need. Anything you can do to minimize the complexity of your program will pay handsome dividends.

The complexity of a program is a function of several factors:

- The number of distinct lexical tokens
- The number of characters
- The number of branches in which control can pass to a different point
- The number of distinct program objects in scope at any time

Whenever a language allows you to change some code to reduce any of these factors, you reduce complexity.

3.7.1 Lose the Temporary Variables

The poster child for complexity is the temporary variable. Any time a language intrudes between you and the solution you visualize, it diminishes your ability to implement the solution. All languages do this to some degree; Perl less than most.[13] In most languages, you swap two variables a and b with the following algorithm:

---

13. We want to say "less than the rest," but we just *know* what sort of letters we'd get . . .

```
Declare temp to be of the same type as a and b
temp = a;
a    = b;
b    = temp;
```

But most languages are not Perl:

```
($b, $a) = ($a, $b);
```

Iterating over an array usually requires an index variable and a count of how many things are currently stored in the array:

```
int i;
for (i = 0; i < count_lines; i++)
    {
    strcat (line[i], suffix);
    }
```

Whereas in Perl, you have the `foreach` construct borrowed from the shell:

```
foreach my $line (@lines) { $line .= $suffix }
```

And if you feel put out by having to type `foreach` instead of just `for`, you're in luck, because they're synonyms for each other; so just type `for` if you want (Perl can tell which one you mean).

Because functions can return lists, you no longer need to build special structures just to return multivalued data. Because Perl does reference-counting garbage collection, you can return variables from the subroutine in which they are created and know that they won't be trampled on, yet their storage will be released later when they're no longer in use. And because Perl doesn't have strong typing of scalars, you can fill a hierarchical data structure with heterogeneous values without having to construct a union datatype and some kind of type descriptor.

Because built-in functions take lists of arguments where it makes sense to do that, you can pass them the results of other functions without having to construct an iterative loop:

```
unlink grep /~$/, readdir DIR;
```

And the `map` function lets you form a new list from an old one with no unnecessary temporary variables:

```
open PASSWD, '/etc/passwd' or die "passwd: $!\n";
my @usernames = map /^([^:]+)/, <PASSWD>;
close PASSWD;
```

Because Perl's arrays grow and shrink automatically and there are simple operators for inserting, modifying, or deleting array elements, you don't need to build linked lists and worry if you've got the traversal termination conditions right. And because Perl has the hash data type, you can quickly locate a particular chunk of information by key or find out whether a member of a set exists.

3.7.2 Scope Out the Problem

Of course, sometimes temporary variables are unavoidable. Whenever you create one though, be sure and do it in the innermost scope possible (in other words, within the most deeply nested set of braces containing all references to the variable).

 Create variables in the innermost scope possible.

For example, let's say somewhere in my program I am traversing my Netscape history file and want to save the URLs visited in the last 10 days in @URLs:

```
use Netscape::History;
my $history = new Netscape::History;
my (@URLs, $url);
```

```
while (defined($url = $history->next_url() ))
   {
   push @URLs, $url if
           time - $url->last_visit_time < 10 * 24 * 3600;
   }
```

This looks quite reasonable on the face of it, but what if later on in our program we create a variable called $history or $url? We'd get the message

```
"my" variable $url masks earlier declaration in same scope
```

which would cause us to search backward in the code to find exactly which one it's referring to. Note the clause "in same scope"—if in the meantime you created a variable $url at a different scope, well, that may be the one you find when searching backward with a text editor, but it won't be the right one. You may have to check your indentation level to see the scope level.

This process could be time-consuming. And really, the problem is in the earlier code, which created the variables $history or $url with far too wide a scope to begin with. We can (as of perl 5.004) put the my declaration of $url right where it is first used in the while statement and thereby limit its scope to the while block. As for $history, we can wrap a bare block around all the code to limit the scope of those variables:

```
use Netscape::History;
my @URLs;
   {
   my $history = new Netscape::History;
   while (defined(my $url = $history->next_url() ))
      {
      push @URLs, $url
         if time - $url->last_visit_time < 10 * 24 * 3600;
      }
   }
```

If you want to create a constant value to use in several places, use con-stant.pm to make sure it can't be overwritten:

```
$PI = 3.1415926535897932384;

use constant PI => 3.1415926535897932384;

my $volume = 4/3 * PI * $radius ** 3;

$PI = 3.0;  # The 'Indiana maneuver' works!
PI  = 3.0;  # But this does not
```

In response to the last statement, Perl returns the error message, "Can't modify constant item in scalar assignment."

constant.pm creates a subroutine of that name which returns the value you've assigned to it, so trying to overwrite it is like trying to assign a value to a subroutine call. Although the absurdity of that may sound like sufficient explanation for how use constant works, in fact, the latest version of perl allows you to assign a value to a subroutine call, provided the result of the subroutine is a place where you could store the value. For example, the subroutine could return a scalar variable. The term for this feature is *lvaluable subroutine*. But since the results of the subroutines created by use constant aren't lvalues, lvaluable subroutines won't cause problems for them.

Chapter 4

Perl Pitfalls

"Is there any point to which you would wish to draw my attention?"

"To the curious incident of the dog in the night-time."

"The dog did nothing in the night-time."

"That was the curious incident," remarked Sherlock Holmes.

Talking with Inspector Gregory, in Silver Blaze, *by Sir Arthur Conan Doyle*

We are not out to "get" Perl in this chapter. Enumerating traps people can fall into when using Perl is like finding technical errors in the movie *Apollo 13*; people do it because they can, whereas with many other languages (or movies), the nits would be too numerous to be worth attempting to pick. What we are going to do is cover some of the places where a little more knowledge would help prevent common errors. You'll find more in the core Perl documentation section `perltrap`.

4.1 Syntactical Sugaring

Perl has an unjustified reputation as a write-only language. We suspect this is because programmers who have never seen it before think they should be able to understand what's going on the first time they lay eyes on a statement the way they could with a BASIC program. But Perl provides many concise idioms and syntactic shortcuts that make programs much shorter than they would have been, and all you need is enough familiarity with the idioms.

4.1.1 The Variable That Wasn't There

A frequent source of bafflement for newcomers is the way that Perl programs seem to be talking to themselves:

```
while (<STDIN>)
   {
   chomp;
   s/#.*//;
   next unless /\S/;
   # ...
   }
```

This apparently defies the usual paradigm of functions operating on variables. What on earth is being operated on?

The answer is the special variable $\$\_$, which is used mainly in its absence. Because it is a default variable for the `chomp`, `s///`, and `m//` functions, and also gets set to the next input line when a readline operator (`<>`) is the only thing inside a `while` clause, that code fragment (which appears to be parsing some data format that can contain embedded comments) can do all kinds of things with and to $\$\_$ without ever having to mention it.

There are plenty of times you *do* have to type $\$\_$, of course. If the previous code needed to add the current line to an array, it would go on to say `push @commands, $_;` since `push` doesn't take a default second argument. As a rule of thumb, the number of implicit references to $\$\_$ should make the explicit references worthwhile; if you have too many explicit references to $\$\_$, then you should probably make them all explicit references to a variable with a useful name. Otherwise you're increasing confusion without having saved enough typing to make it worth it.

12 **If you have many explicit references to the same instance of $\$\_$, use a named variable instead.**

There are also times when it's feasible to use $\$\_$ but not worth the trouble. For instance, if you're nesting one loop that uses $\$\_$ as the loop variable around another, such as:

```
my @list = qw(alpha);
$_ = "aleph";
foreach (@list)
    {
    while (<STDIN>)
        {
        # do something
        }
    }
```

When the smoke clears from feeding values to the loop reading lines from `STDIN`, what value will $\$\_$ have? If you answered `"aleph"`, reasoning that $\$\_$ should have been saved while you were going around the loops, congratulations, you're right. But before you head off to celebrate, take a look at the contents of @list. It still contains one element, but its value is now undef instead of "alpha". Oops.

The reason is that the foreach loop *aliased* $_ to each element of its list in turn. Therefore anything done to $_ would get done to that array element.[1] And while the foreach loop saved (or *localized*) its loop variable of $_, the while loop didn't. So when it read a line from STDIN, it did so into the same $_ in use by foreach, which overwrote the array element.

Yuck! What can we do about this? Is the solution to say that you shouldn't nest one loop that uses $_ as the loop variable inside another? Consider the following:

```
sub proc
   {
   while (<STDIN>)
      {
      # do something
      }
   }
```

Now do we have to check every place that calls proc() and its ancestors to see if it's inside a foreach loop? Hardly.

What we can do is remember that while is the only loop statement that doesn't localize $_, so we just need to do it ourselves whenever we construct a while statement that might end up in a context where $_ is already in use:

```
sub proc
   {
   local $_;
   while (<STDIN>)
      {
```

---

1. Because it's writable. Trying to change an aliased list element that isn't an lvalue triggers the error "Modification of a read-only value attempted."

```
    # do something
    }
}
```

Now you can safely call `proc()` from within a `foreach` loop to your heart's content.

 When using a `while` loop that sets $_, localize $_ first if it might be called from elsewhere.

Note that when we say *localize*, this really does call for the `local` operator, which we otherwise prefer to avoid. Reason: you can't make a lexical $_ with `my`, because it's a special pseudo-global variable that just won't stand for possessiveness.

4.1.2 The Case of the Vanishing Parentheses

Unlike practically every other procedural language in existence, when you call a function or procedure in Perl (both of which are just "subroutines" in Perl parlance), it is not always necessary to put its arguments inside parentheses. If Perl can tell what the arguments are without the parentheses, you don't have to put them in. This makes for more readable code, not to mention less typing; for instance

```
print join ' ', reverse split /:/;
```

is arguably more aesthetic than

```
print(join(' ', reverse(split(/:/))));
```

and stops you from feeling like you're typing LISP.

On the other hand, be careful not to leave them out when they're necessary:

```
my %userdb = (pjscott => "Peter Scott",
              ewright => "Ed Wright");
print "Usernames: ", join " ", sort keys %userdb, "\n";
```

results in

```
Usernames:
 ewright pjscott
```

with no newline on the end. This happens because the prototype for `sort` is

> `sort` optional_subroutine_or_block *LIST*

and so how is Perl to know where the LIST ends? As long as there are terms that look like list elements, they'll get included, and that means the `"\n"` is sorted along with the hash keys. So you'll actually have to bend your fingers over to the parentheses keys in this case and type

```
print "Usernames: ", join " ", sort (keys %userdb), "\n";
```

In fact, there's more than one way to do this, and it's instructive to look at some of the other possibilities:

```
print "Usernames: ", join " ", (sort keys %userdb), "\n";
print "Usernames: ", join (" ", sort keys %userdb), "\n";
print "Usernames: ", (join " ", sort keys %userdb), "\n";
```

We're using two different ways of limiting the scope of the `sort` arguments here. One is to put the arguments to a function in parentheses; the other is to put the function name along with its arguments in parentheses. We get the same result by two different means: When the function arguments are contained in parentheses, Perl exercises a parsing rule called "if-it-looks-like-a-function-then-it-is-a-function," and the parentheses delineate the function argument list. When the function and its arguments are contained within parentheses, the parentheses create a term, keeping the `sort` from consuming any arguments outside the term (see Table 4-1 in section 4.2).

What about this:

```
print ("Usernames: ", join " ", sort keys %userdb), "\n";
```

If you try this without the $-w$ flag, you'll see that the newline isn't printed. If you put the $-w$ flag in, you find out why:

```
print (...) interpreted as function at line 1.
Useless use of a constant in void context at line 1.
```

The reason for this is apparent from the rules we've already stated: Perl is exercising the if-it-looks-like-a-function-then-it-is-a-function rule, which means that the arguments to the print function are contained within the parentheses, and what follows is a comma operator and a constant. Since that constant isn't being assigned or passed to anything, it serves no purpose, and Perl warns us that we're putting a constant in a place where it does nothing.[2]

If you find yourself confronting that warning but you really did mean what you said and you want the warning to go away, you can put a + in front of the parentheses:

```
print +("Usernames: ", join " ", sort keys %userdb), "\n";
```

which doesn't change what gets printed but does create the interpretation you want. Usually, however, nothing so unintuitive is called for. If you want to exccute multiple statements without having to put them in a block, the low-precedence logical and is perfect:

```
warn "We're out of $food\n" and return
    unless exists $menu{$food};
```

This doesn't need any parentheses at all. (But make sure the statement before the and is bound to evaluate as true.)

---

2. If you're wondering why Perl doesn't raise a similar objection to the "1" that you should put at the end of a module that gets used or required, the answer is that it is at the end of a notional block— the file itself—and therefore gets parsed as a return value.

Here's another example of the same problem: trying to populate a hash from an array with this:

```
my @nums = 1..100;
my %square = map ($_, $_ * $_), @nums;
```

causes the complaint `Useless use of private array in void context` because while the programmer wanted the `map` expression to return a two-element list, the looks-like-a-function rule made the first argument `$_` and the second argument `$_ * $_`, thereby leaving poor `@nums` out in the cold, hard space of void context. This also can be cured by placing a + in front of the parentheses.

One place it helps to put parentheses in is where you're passing no arguments to a function that can take some. Consider a subroutine for converting Fahrenheit to Celsius:

```
use constant RATIO => 9/5;
sub c2f
   {
   return shift * RATIO + 32;
   }
```

Compile this and you'll see

```
Type of arg 1 to shift must be array (not addition (+))
```

Incidentally, if you parenthesize it as `return (shift * RATIO) + 32;` you get an even more interesting error,

```
Type of arg 1 to shift must be array (not ref-to-glob cast)
```

What's happening is that Perl thinks that what follows `shift` may be an argument for it, since it looks like the beginning of a token that could be one.

With experience—or table 3-3, "Ambiguous Characters" in the third edition of *Programming Perl* (Wall, et al., O'Reilly, 2000)—you'll learn where you don't need to apply this solution:

Put empty parentheses after a function that could take arguments but doesn't.[3]

In particular, it's always safe to leave them off if the function call is the last thing in the statement.

4.1.3 The Many Faces of { }

When you think about the myriad uses of braces,[4] it's amazing that Perl can keep them all straight. They're used for delineating code blocks, hash keys, anonymous hash references, and regular expression quantifiers, and can also be used as delimiters for the q, qq, qr, qw, qx, m//, s///, and tr// operators. Those code blocks are used in many places, like subroutine declarations, sort or map routines, or even part of a variable identifier:

```
print "Three largest cities:
    @{$state_info{NY}{Megalopoles}}[0..2]";
```

The amazing thing is that Perl has so many uses for braces yet hardly ever needs help telling which one you mean. Because there are so many ways in which braces are valid in Perl, though, incorrect use may generate no message or something cryptic. The most common brace mistake for newcomers is hash initializations:

```
my %queen = { Britain     => 'Elizabeth',
              Netherlands => 'Beatrix' };  # Wrong!
```

This is so common that it is specifically checked for by -w, which gives the warning Reference found where even-sized list expected.

---

3. There is one ugly exception to this rule, the eof function. If you ever need to use it, look in perlfunc first to see what we mean.

4. In Perl. We don't want to know what else you use something for holding your pants or your teeth together.

(No message is output without -w; before you get much further in this book you will be convinced that no Perl program should be allowed to run without it.)

This isn't an outright error, because it is, in fact, syntactically valid: it creates a hash with one key for which the value is undef. That key is the stringified form of a reference to an anonymous hash, so it looks something like "HASH(0xbd864)." The anonymous hash it refers to is the one the newcomer intended to create but got confused about when to use braces in connection with hashes. (The right-hand side should be a list, and literal lists are surrounded by parentheses.)

The most common place where necessary braces are omitted is in dereferencing compound constructs such as the "three largest cities" example. If we'd left out one set of braces and written the variable as

```
@$state_info{NY}{Megalopoles}[0..2]
```

we would have triggered the compilation error

```
Can't use subscript on hash slice
```

which gives us a clue that Perl is trying to parse it as though it were

```
@{$state_info}{NY}{Megalopoles}[0..2]
```

which means, "Treat $state_info as a reference to a hash, return the slice of that hash with the single key NY, then take the element of that with the key Megalopoles—whoa, the thing we're trying to subscript is not a hash!"

4.2 The Hall of the Precedence

Perl has a complicated precedence ordering; it helps to be able to look it up quickly (fortunately, it's the first thing out of perldoc perlop). We reproduce that table here (Table 4-1) because we'll be referring to it.

TABLE 4-1. Perl Operator Precedence and Associativity

Associativity	Operators
Left	Terms and list operators (leftward)
Left	->
Nonassoc	++ --
Right	**
Right	! ~ \ and unary + and -
Left	=~ !~
Left	* / % x
Left	+ - .
Left	<< >>
Nonassoc	Named unary and file test operators
Nonassoc	< > <= >= lt gt le ge
Nonassoc	== != <=> eq ne cmp
Left	&
Left	| ^
Left	&&
Left	||
Nonassoc	.. ...
Right	?:
Right	= op=
Left	, =>
Nonassoc	List operators (rightward)
Right	not
Left	and
Left	or xor

Associativity tells you what order to evaluate multiple operators of the same precedence appearing together in an expression. So the arithmetic expression 3 − 4 + 5 is evaluated as (3 − 4) + 5 because while − and + have the same precedence, they are left-associative, meaning that left-most elements take precedence over right-most elements. "Nonassoc" means that the operators don't associate; in other words, you can't have more than one in a row without parentheses to create a valid meaning. So while some languages let you write[5]

```
if (0 <= $percent <= 100)
```

Perl isn't one of them.[6]

As the `perlop` manual page says, "Operators borrowed from C keep the same precedence relationship with each other, even where C's precedence is slightly screwy." It turns out that some of the precedence rules for C were chosen to match those of its predecessor B, even where *those* were slightly screwy. (Backward compatibility has its pitfalls.)

So most of the precedence gotchas in C are inherited by Perl. For instance, if you're checking a variable that contains a selection of flags logically ORed together against a candidate (as we will do in Chapter 5), the line

```
warn "Database opened\n" if ($opt_D & $DB_LOG != 0)
```

has an unfortunate flaw, because it is evaluated as

```
warn "Database opened\n" if ($opt_D & ($DB_LOG != 0))
```

So if, for instance, $opt_D was 6, and $DB_LOG was 2, the `warn` statement would be incorrectly omitted since 2 != 0 evaluates to 1, and 1 & 6 is 0, which is false.

---

5. One of the first languages Peter learned was BCPL, which allowed this.
6. Yet. It's been mooted for Perl 6.

The cure lies in simplicity:

```
warn "Database opened\n" if ($opt_D & $DB_LOG)
```

at the cost of infinitesimal clarity.

Here's another example of precedence combined with optional parentheses around function arguments getting us into trouble:

```
vec $v, $offset, 32 = 1;   # Wrong
```

The programmer who thought that since the prototype for `vec` is $$$ that the processing of its arguments would terminate after 32 failed to realize that $=$ has a higher precedence than the commas separating list arguments. Therefore Perl parses it as:

```
vec($v, $offset, (32 = 1));
```

and emits the error

```
Can't modify constant item in scalar assignment.
```

What other precedence pitfalls pursue Perl programmers? A few follow.

4.2.1 Regex Binding

Let's say that you want to check whether the next element of an array matches a regular expression, and you write

```
if (shift @marsupials =~
          /platypus|wallaby|(kanga)?roo|joey/) ...
```

This results in a warning (with −w) and an error:

```
Applying pattern match to @array will act on scalar(@array)..
Type of arg 1 to shift must be array (not pattern match)...
```

Reason: the binding operator =~ is above "named unary operators" in Table 4-1. So it tries to bind the regex to @marsupials (which must put the array in scalar context, hence the warning), and then shift the result of the regex match (which results in the error).

Fortunately, there are so many ways of coding this right that this is an unlikely pitfall to encounter by accident. Like all precedence misunderstandings, inserting parentheses is one way to fix it:

```
if (shift(@marsupials) =~
            /platypus|wallaby|(kanga)?roo|joey/)
```

Use parentheses when in doubt about precedence; they won't hurt.

4.2.2 Arithmetic on **keys**

Suppose you have a hash %h and you want to find out how many elements are in it, so you type:

```
print "Number of elements: " . keys %h . "\n";
```

reasoning with impeccable logic that the dots will force keys into scalar context and therefore return the number of keys in %h instead of the list of them. However, Perl responds with

```
Type of arg 1 to keys must be hash (not concatenation)
```

A quick glance at Table 4-1 shows us that "named unary operators" rank below the . operator in precedence; therefore Perl parses the statement as

```
print "Number of elements: " . keys (%h."\n");
```

which, unsurprisingly, makes no more sense to Perl than it does to us. We can fix it easily enough by leaving the first dot in and turning the second one into a comma:

```
print "Number of elements: " . keys %h, "\n";
```

(This comma is evaluated as the low-precedence "list operators (right-ward)" element from Table 4-1.) We can generalize this to all the other named unary operators (functions prototyped to take a single argument), of course. Peruse the `perlfunc` manual page to find out what those are.

4.3 Regular Expressions

You may be accustomed to using `s//A New Beginning/` to insert some text at the beginning of the current line in some applications. In Perl (as in `sed`), the empty regular expression doesn't match a zero-length substring; it matches whatever the previous regular expression matched. If there isn't a previous regular expression, Perl and `sed` part company: Perl treats it as matching the beginning of the string; `sed` says it's an error.

4.4 Miscellaneous

4.4.1 Autovivification

You wouldn't ordinarily expect to alter the value of something just by looking at it. So when that happens (even if for very good reasons), it's worth drawing attention to it so you can look out for it.

Autovivification is an expensive Perl term that you can impress your friends with. It means that certain variables get created for you if necessary. Perl has extremely friendly syntax for creating multidimensional data structures. For instance, let's say you're populating the hash `%state_info` from section 4.1.3; you have first-level keys that are state abbreviations and second-level keys that are names of state attributes, one of which names the largest cities. You can insert the entry for those cities right off the bat:

```
$state_info{NY}{Megalopoles} = ['New York',
                                'Albany',
                                'Rochester'];
```

What's remarkable about this is how easy it is. A C programmer getting to know Perl would look at this and say, "Er, don't you need to at least insert a reference to a hash in the first-level value before this...?" What they mean is, the preceding code reveals that the values of `%state_info` are references to hashes; if `$state_info{NY}` doesn't exist yet, then why doesn't the assignment above blow up when it tries to dereference an undefined value to find where the value for the second-level key `Megalopoles` is? To do the same in C, a programmer would first have to `malloc` a new `state_info` struct with a field of `NY`, insert it into a binary tree, `malloc` another struct with a field of `Megalopoles`, insert a pointer to it in the previous struct, then `malloc` three more structs with the city names, link them into a list, and put a pointer to the head of the list in the `Megalopoles` struct. Pant, pant.

That Perl doesn't do this is another example of its philosophy of, "Don't throw an exception if you can do something useful." When the assignment above is executed, Perl will look to see if there is a key `NY` in the `%state_info` hash; if there isn't (or if there is but the corresponding value is `undef`), it will create one with a value containing a reference to an anonymous hash with a key `Megalopoles` and a value of a reference to an anonymous array containing the three listed cities. Now you know what autovivification is.

What does this have to do with the Heisenbergian lead-in to this section? Well, sometimes when you're just looking to see if a second- (or third-, etc.) level hash key exists, Perl can't help but create a first-level value through this autovivification process. For instance,

```
my %state_info;    # So you know it's empty at this point
print "The Big Apple is here!\n"
    if exists $state_info{NY}{Megalopoles};
use Data::Dumper;
print Dumper \%state_info;
```

prints

```
$VAR1 = {
          'NY' => {}
        };
```

In other words, just looking to see whether the key `Megalopoles` existed caused Perl to autovivify the intermediate hash. The documentation says that this behavior may be fixed in a future release of Perl, but it also appears to be extremely hard to do so.

16 **Before testing the existence of a lower-level hash key, test the existence of the higher-level keys if there's a chance they may be absent.**

We'll talk more about the useful `Data::Dumper` module in Chapter 5.

4.4.2 `split`

The `split` function deserves its own section. It has almost enough special cases to qualify as its own programming language. Our first potential gotcha emerges when we're validating a Unix `passwd` file for the correct number of fields on each line:

```
@ARGV = '/etc/passwd';
while (<>)
   {
   print "Wrong # of fields in line $.\n"
     unless split /:/ == 7;
   }
```

Our first problem is that this does't find any of the lines that have the wrong number of fields; it silently fails. We've just created another precedence problem: referring back to Table 4-1, we see that list operators have a lower precedence than the == operator, and `split` is a list operator; therefore we've just given it a first argument of `/:/ == 7`.

By changing the `unless` clause to `split(/:/) == 7`, we create working code, but, alas, not silent code. With warnings enabled, perl prints `Use of implicit split to @_ is deprecated` because `split` in a scalar context for legacy reasons puts its result into the `@_` array, and this is behavior that the Perl maintainers would like to eliminate one day.

We do not want our code to cause warnings, however benign.

 Eliminate all causes of warning messages in a program before proceeding with further development.

Clearly we cannot call `split` in a scalar context without causing the warning; therefore we have two choices: either disable warnings:

```
@ARGV = '/etc/passwd';
while (<>)
    {
    local $^W;  # Set warning flag to undef for this block
    print "Error on line $.\n" unless split /:/ == 7;
    }
```

or call it in a list context:[7]

```
@ARGV = '/etc/passwd';
while (<>)
    {
    my @split = split /:/;
    print "Error on line $.\n" unless @split == 7;
    }
```

A common `split` mistake is to supply a string literal as the first argument and expect it to split on that string. However, the argument is still interpreted as a regular expression and if it contains metacharacters, the behavior is unex-

---

7. If you want to do this without using a temporary variable, we applaud the sentiment. However, the solution is `print "Error on line $.\n" unless (() = split (/:/, $_, 7))  == 7`, which is anything but sentimental.

pected. The most common occurrence of this appears to be trying to use `split '|'` to split on a vertical bar (which makes a good field separator), but instead it is interpreted as regex alternation and winds up splitting on every character.

The other `split` gotcha we want to bring to your attention is the behavior of a pattern of `//`. Anywhere else you used a regex of `//`, it would mean, "Repeat the last regular expression" (which is another gotcha). But in a `split`, that pattern always means, "Split the string into separate characters."

4.4.3 Reserved Words

Perl reserves a few words in all capital letters to itself for various reasons. The full list is large but includes many identifiers used only as subroutines in tied classes, which won't get in your way. Here are the rest:

- AUTOLOAD
- BEGIN
- CHECK
- CORE
- DATA
- DESTROY
- END
- GLOBAL
- INIT

The following still exist in 5.6.0 but are deprecated and unlikely to be in the next version:

- EQ, GE, GT, LE, LT, NE

Different rules govern the contexts in which each of these is given its special interpretation; the wisest course of action is not to use any of them for the customary uses of all-caps words:

- Constants created with `use constant`
- Filehandles
- Loop labels

You should not name any subroutine with all capital letters, because it has a far greater chance of being interpreted as a special Perl routine if the names are the same. From perl 5.6.0 onwards, filehandles can be put into scalars with `open my $fh, $filename;` which is much cleaner than using the FILE-HANDLE syntax, especially if you want to pass `$fh` to a subroutine.

On a related note, be aware of the names of Perl's built-in functions (`perldoc perlfunc`), or you could run into this situation:

```perl
#!/usr/bin/perl -wl
use strict;

sub sin
    {
    (qw(Pride Envy Gluttony Lust Anger
        Greed Sloth Obfuscation))[$_[0]+1];
    }
print sin(5);
```

which produces

```
Ambiguous call resolved as CORE::sin(), qualify as such or use &
at ./sin line 9.
-0.958924274663138
```

Perl found a conflict between the subroutine you declared and its built-in function `sin` (which does something rather different) and resolved it in favor of the latter. Worse yet, if we had declared our version of `sin` *after* the call we made to it, while this normally wouldn't matter, in this case it would mean we wouldn't even get the ambiguity warning.[8]

---

8. In other words, there's just no escaping the original sin.

There are several things we can do about this possibility. First, we can become familiar with Perl's built-in function names so that we don't give a subroutine the same name as one. Second, we can declare our subroutines before the code that uses them. Note we say *declare*, not *define:* you can insert a forward declaration anywhere by omitting the code block. This also lets you use subroutine prototypes:

```
sub version ($$);    # Declares
# Time passes...
version (1, 5);
# More time passes...
sub version ($$)     # Defines
   {
   my ($major, $minor) = @_;
   #...
   }
```

Third, we could call all our own subroutines with an & prefix, which will prevent confusion with a built-in. We don't like this solution personally, because it's visually less appealing to us, but it could be very useful to a new-comer.

18 **Declare subroutines early, avoid collisions with the Perl built-in functions, or call them with &.**

4.4.4 Secret Prototypes

Our next pitfall concerns the "secret" function prototypes assigned to built-in functions. If you execute the following:

```
my     @arglist = ("My %s has %d %s\n");
push   @arglist, 'aunt', 3, 'cats';
printf @arglist;
print  sprintf @arglist;
```

(not that you would do something so strange, but we're illustrating something that you might come across more circuitously), the result is

```
My aunt has 3 cats
4
```

What's going on? The first line is right, so what happened with the second one?

`sprintf()` has an implicit *prototype*. If you'd written `sprintf` yourself,[9] you'd have begun it with

```
sub sprintf ($@)
```

which is a somewhat contentious feature of Perl that allows you to emulate the ability of built-in functions to dispense with parentheses around their arguments if you so wish.

Well, it allows you to emulate *some* built-in functions, but we'll get to that.

This prototype says that `sprintf` takes a scalar (either a variable or a literal expression) followed by a list. The first argument will therefore be interpreted in scalar context. And the first (and only) argument we passed in our example was `@arglist`, which in a scalar context yields the number of elements in the array: 4.

"Okay," you say, licking your wounds but determined to come back fighting, "so why didn't the same problem occur with `printf`? What's the difference?"

The difference is that `printf` wasn't given the same internal prototype. (This may be changed in a later version of perl.) But in the case of `printf`, you couldn't write a prototype for it yourself if your life depended on it, because `printf` can take a filehandle as a special kind of first argument:

```
printf STDOUT "The answer is %d\n", 42;
```

---

9. Always an enjoyable way to spend a rainy afternoon.

Note there's no comma after it! The prototyping mechanism available to mere *users* of perl does not permit this.)

Most of the built-in ("core") functions in Perl have implicit prototypes. As of version 5.005, you can find out what they are with the `prototype` function and prefixing the built-in with the string `"CORE::"`.[10] For example:

```
$ perl -le 'print prototype "CORE::substr"'
$$;$;$
```

A `$` indicates a scalar is expected, and a `;` means that the following argument is optional. If you compare this with the `perlfunc` entry for `substr`, you'll see that it can take two, three, or four scalar arguments. If a function is so special that you couldn't write a prototype for it (like `printf`), `prototype` returns `undef`.

It's unlikely that you'll trip over anything besides `sprintf`, because the other prototypes for built-ins are such that if you passed an array where Perl was expecting some scalars, you'd get a compile-time error that there weren't enough function arguments. And this is the reason those prototypes exist: to tell you at compile time that you haven't provided enough arguments to a routine.

Unfortunately there is a trade-off at work here: if you want to make sure the user provides two scalars as function arguments (like the built-in `crypt`) and throw a compile-time exception if they don't, then you should declare that function with a prototype of `$$`. But then the user can't supply an array containing two arguments to the function and get the result they want. (There again, what are the odds someone would want to supply the two arguments to `crypt` via an array?) Whether or not *you* use subroutine prototypes, be aware that most of the perl built-ins do, and that the Perl porters consider `printf` to be the interface in need of repair, not `sprintf`, regardless of what happened in our contrived example.

---

10. As you might have guessed, `prototype` can be used to discover prototypes for any function, not just built-ins.

If you wanted to make a more general rule out of this nitpicky point, the Perl of Wisdom would be

19 **Don't pass arrays to built-in functions which normally expect a scalar.**

4.4.5 Loop Scope

After a `for` loop, the loop variable has the last value it was set to (unless it was lexically scoped to the loop itself, in which case it no longer exists). But after a `foreach` loop (one that doesn't lexically scope the variable to itself), the variable has the value it had *before* the loop:

```
$ perl -le 'my $i = 42; for ($i=0; $i<10; $i++) {} print $i'
10
$ perl -le 'my $i = 42; foreach $i (1..10) {} print $i'
42
```

This can be particularly nonintuitive if you break out of the `foreach` loop with `last` because you've found the thing you were looking for.

20 **Don't rely on loop variables retaining their values after the loop; save them explicitly if you need them.**

Chapter 5

Tracing Code

"1545 Relay #70 Panel F (moth) in relay.

First actual case of bug being found."

Admiral Grace Hopper's Logbook
September 9, 1945

In the phylogeny of debugging, the Protozoic approach consists of tossing

```
print "\$variable = $variable\n";
```

lines into the problem code at various places. Before we advance up the evolutionary ladder to interactive debuggers in Chapter 7, however, we have a lot of ground to cover.

We should not so readily disparage the humble `print` statement, because with a little tuning it can turn into a valuable tool. As we've already seen, the most basic kind of tracing statement prints out a variable name and its value. You can improve on it slightly by printing to STDERR instead of the currently selected filehandle.[1] It's also a good idea to make it stand out so that you remember to remove it when you're done debugging:

```
print STDERR "***DEBUG*** \@names = @names\n";
```

When you put an array in string context like that, it turns it into a string of all the array elements separated by spaces.[2] We find that trace statements like this are our major use of this feature.

If you want to economize on keystrokes, you can say `warn` instead:[3]

```
warn "***DEBUG*** Usernames: ", values %username, "\n";
```

By sending your tracing output to STDERR, you have left undisturbed the normal output of your program to STDOUT, which means it can continue to run as a command in a pipeline sequence if you so desire. You can also output status information to STDERR in such a program (sometimes called a *filter*).

---

1. Or even create a separate filehandle DEBUG for debugging output and redirect it wherever you want as development proceeds.

2. Actually, separated by the value of the `$"` variable, which you can change if you want.

3. The only way this would differ from `print`ing to STDERR is if you happen to have installed a `__WARN__` handler, in which case, presumably, you know what you're doing.

It's a good idea in this case to identify your program so that you can tell which command in the pipeline is talking to you:

```
% grep -li pseudo-hash /usr/local/perl/man/man1/*     \
  | mytran | mail -s "Secrets you requested, tovarich" \
  gyorgi@kgb.moskvax.ru
mytran: Translating /usr/local/perl/man/man1/perldelta.1 into
Russian...
mytran: ***DEBUG*** $trans{perl} => 'zhemchuzhina'
mytran: Translating /usr/local/perl/man/man1/perldiag.1 into
Russian...
[...]
```

You do that by inserting $0 in your output string. $0 is the string with which your program was invoked. Note that this may include leading components of an absolute or relative path, so you may want to strip off everything before the filename component. The operating system-independent way to do this is:

```
use File::Basename;
my $prog = fileparse($0);
# $prog now contains the program name along with any suffix
```

5.1 Dumping Your Data

That is all well and good for scalars and arrays, but it won't even handle hashes, let alone complex lists of lists. A good way to deal with those is to use the Dumper function in the Data::Dumper module which will let you print out, nicely formatted, anything you give it, no matter how complex:

```
use Data::Dumper;
# set %state from some database or flat file
warn Dumper(\%state);
```

which produces

```
$VAR1 = {
        'WI' => {
                'BIRD'          => 'Robin',
                'NAME'          => 'Wisconsin',
                'LARGEST_CITY' => 'Milwaukee',
                'CAPITAL'       => 'Madison',
                'FLOWER'        => 'Wood Violet'
        },
        'MS' => {
                'BIRD'          => 'Mockingbird',
                'NAME'          => 'Mississippi',
                'LARGEST_CITY' => 'Jackson',
                'CAPITAL'       => 'Jackson',
                'FLOWER'        => 'Magnolia'
        },
[...]
```

Note that we passed a reference to the hash we were examining to `Dumper`. If we were to pass the hash itself, all the elements of the hash `%state` would become a list input to the routine, and each would be displayed as though it were a separate variable (hence given the labels `$VAR1`, `$VAR2`, etc.). By passing a reference to `%state`, `Dumper` sees just the one variable, a reference to a hash, and can format its output as keys and associated values. `Dumper` can also detect references it has previously followed and thus minimize the size of the output necessary (and avoid problems with circular references).

 Use the `Data::Dumper` module to print out a formatted dump of any variable or hierarchical data structure.

5.2 Making it Optional

After typing in a tracing statement, taking it out after the code is "working," then putting it back in when the code mysteriously stops working, you're motivated to find a way to leave it in there and selectively enable it.

The most primitive way is to comment it out, but since there are no independently compiled binary executables for Perl programs,[4] this isn't as bad a solution as it would be for, say, C—you'd have to rebuild the executable and have a way of knowing whether it was in sync with the source. Just make sure that if your `print` statement exceeds one line, you comment/uncomment all the lines.

The next most basic option is to create a program-wide Boolean variable that controls whether your tracing statements are executed: this is an acceptable use of a global variable.

```
use constant DEBUG => 1;
# later that same program...
warn "***DEBUG*** Tax rate = $tax_rate\n" if DEBUG;
```

Note that we made `DEBUG` a constant so it doesn't accidentally get overwritten elsewhere.

With enough such `warn` statements in your code the Laziness Principle will assert itself:

```
use constant DEBUG => 1;
sub dbgprt (@);

# code ...

dbgprt "$. lines in input file\n";

# more code ...

sub dbgprt (@)
   {
   warn "***DEBUG*** ", @_ if DEBUG;
   }
```

---

4. With a few qualification-ridden exceptions.

Now we've abstracted all the functionality we might want to change about our tracing statements (what marker text they use, how to decide whether to print them, what output function they use) into one place where we need to change it only once. We've created a prototype for the `dbgprt` subroutine before its first use so that we can use it the same way as we do `warn` (in this case, passing it a list of arguments without having to put parentheses around them).

Fully evolved, you say? *Au contraire,* we've merely advanced to the aquatic stage. If we really want to walk on the land, it's time to find our feet.

5.3 Raise the Flag

Our option so far is binary: either we print a tracing statement or we don't. But suppose we want to discriminate and print some tracing statements at some times, and others at other times. Perhaps we want to preserve our earliest tracing statements; even though we suspect they've become redundant now that the code around them is working, we want to keep them around. Fair enough. We can create classes of tracing statement and assign a number to each one:

Number	Statement Class
1	The very first tracing statements we entered
2	The next tracing statements we entered, which we want to keep distinct
4	Another set of statements that are distinct from 1 and 2

And so on. The numbering scheme is not random: by using successive powers of two, it allows us to specify any combination of flags in a single number.[5] Now the DEBUG constant is no longer a Boolean:

```
use constant DEBUG => 1 | 4;   # Choose classes 1 and 4
sub dbgprt ($@);
```

---

5. As long as we don't exceed the number of bits in an integer.

```
# code ...

dbgprt 2, "DTD schema = $dtd\n";

# more code ...

sub dbgprt ($@)
   {
   my $class = shift;
   warn "***DEBUG*** ", @_ if DEBUG & $class;
   }
```

By logically ORing (|) together the numbers that represent the classes we want printed, we can create one number that represents a set. Now each tracing statement passes the debug class number as the first parameter to dbgprt, which just logically ANDs it with thc DEBUG constant; if the result is not zero, that class number was requested, and therefore the statement will print.

These aren't terribly useful debug class identifiers, though. They might mean something to us, but chances are they won't help the next person who takes over our code. And as your code matures, rather than assign debug classes in chronological order, you should distinguish them on the basis of some logical functionality instead. So let's use symbolic names instead, and figure out a title for each class. Let's say we're writing a shopping cart program that interfaces with CGI scripts and a corporate database:

Identifier	Statement Class
WEB	Statements about Web connections
SQL	Statements containing SQL statements to be submitted to the database
REG	Statements about the customer registry

This requires very little change:

```
use constant WEB => 1;
use constant SQL => 2;
use constant REG => 4;
```

```
use constant DEBUG => WEB | REG;  # Choose these classes

sub dbgprt ($@);

# code ...

dbgprt WEB, "Using port $port on server $server\n";

# more code ...

sub dbgprt ($@)
   {
   my $class = shift;
   warn "***DEBUG*** ", @_ if DEBUG & $class;
   }
```

You might find it useful to include the message class in the output also. Then you can search your log files later on for certain message classes.

5.4 At Your Command

It would be better to have the option to change the combination of debug flags at run time rather than having to change the source each time we want different output.

 Migrate option setting to the most convenient input interface possible.

In other words, when you have an option that can be changed, the least desirable place to do it is in the source code (within which there are better and worse ways of doing it, as we have discussed); the next best choice is an input configuration file (if your program supports one), an environment variable, or a command line option. Many people write programs that support all four methods with each one being overridden by the next. We'll just demonstrate how to set debug flags from the command line, falling back to the source code.

```
use constant WEB => 1;
use constant SQL => 2;
use constant REG => 4;
use Getopts::Std;
use vars qw($opt_D);

$opt_D = WEB | REG;  # Default

sub dbgprt ($@);
getopts('D:') or die &usage;

# code ...

dbgprt SQL, "Query returned $rows rows\n";

# more code ...

sub dbgprt ($@)
   {
   my $class = shift;
   warn "***DEBUG*** ", @_ if $opt_D & $class;
   }
```

We can now call our program with the command line option −D, followed by the number resulting from ORing all our desired options:[6]

```
% whizzbang.pl -D 5    # Set WEB and REG options
```

Later in our program we include a `usage` subroutine that returns a string telling the user how they should really call this program if they made a mistake. If this program takes other command line options—a distinct possibility—then their letters will be added to the `getopts` call.

Hmm, wouldn't it be nice if we could set them from the command line symbolically as well? Say, with something like

---

6. Of course, e-commerce middleware is unlikely to be started from the command line or to log its output to the terminal, but those are orthogonal issues.

```
% whizzbang.pl -D WEB,REG
```

Now we've not only decoupled the interface from the constant definitions in the source, but we've done away with the need for the comment. Easy enough:

```perl
use constant WEB => 1;
use constant SQL => 2;
use constant REG => 4;
my %dbg_flag = (
    WEB => WEB,
    SQL => SQL,
    REG => REG);

use Getopt::Std;
use vars qw($opt_D);

my $DEBUG = WEB | REG;  # Default

sub dbgprt ($@);
getopts('D:') or die &usage;

if ($opt_D)
    {
    $DEBUG = 0;
    $DEBUG |= $dbg_flag{uc $_}
            || die "Unknown debug flag $_\n"
        foreach split /,/, $opt_D;
    }

# code ...

dbgprt REG, "User $username has \$$bal left in account\n";

# more code ...

sub dbgprt ($@)
    {
    my $class = shift;
    warn "***DEBUG*** ", @_  if $DEBUG & $class;
    }
```

There's nothing to be intimidated by here. First, we've added a hash `%dbg_flag` that maps the symbolic names to their values. We wisely chose the strings that we're accepting as input to have the same names as the symbolic constants in our source code, so the hash initialization becomes extremely easy to maintain (the keys on the left are barewords that get converted to strings without the need for quoting because we're using the => operator to do it for us).

Then we set a default for `$DEBUG`, our variable holding the set of debug message classes to print, and checked to see whether `$opt_D` was set, which it would be only if the user put it on the command line. If it was, then we logically ORed together the values in the hash whose keys are each string between commas in the option value and, of course, provided feedback if the user specified an incorrect one.

5.5 *Taking the Long Way Around*

There's an alternative way of option parsing using the core module `Getopt::Long`:

```
use Getopt::Long;
use constant WEB => 1;
use constant SQL => 2;
use constant REG => 4;

my %dbg_flag = (
    WEB => WEB,
    SQL => SQL,
    REG => REG);
my %dbg;

GetOptions(\%dbg, "D=s@");
my $DEBUG = WEB | REG unless $dbg{D};

$DEBUG |= $dbg_flag{$_}
      || die "Unknown debug flag $_\n"
    foreach @{$dbg{D}};
```

(We've shown only the option-parsing part.) This has a slightly different interface; instead of separating multiple values with commas, we must repeat the `-D` flag:

```
% whizzbang.pl -D WEB -D REG
```

(We could also say "`-D=WEB -D=REG`".)

`Getopt::Long` permits many more choices than this, of course. If you have a complex program (particularly one worked on by multiple programmers), look to it for support for the kind of debug flag setting interface you'll find useful. Brad Appleton says

> Sometimes I will have a debug flag per each important subsystem of a large Perl program encompassing many modules. Each one will have an integer value. Sometimes I will have a debug argument along the lines of
>
> ```
> -debug Pkg1=f1,f2,... -debug Pkg2=f3,f4,...
> ```
>
> If the value for `Pkg1` is an integer, it sets a package-wide debug level/flag. Otherwise, it says which specific functions to debug in the package.

If you've been thinking that "tracing code" means profiling its run-time performance, never fear; we will tackle that topic in Chapter 11.

Chapter 6

Testing Perl Programs

"Run and find out."

The Jungle Book, Rikki-Tikki-Tavi *by Rudyard Kipling*

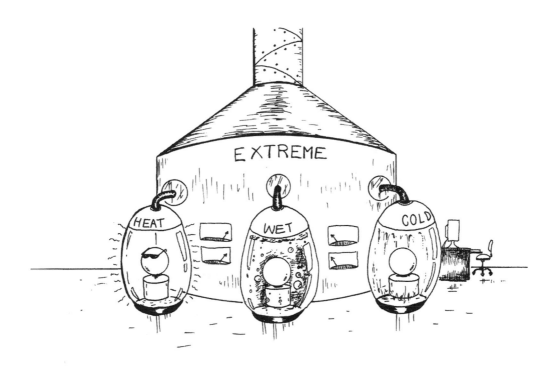

Hands up everyone who hates testing their code. Yes, we thought so. And who can blame you? The hidden beliefs that make testing so painful run deep:

- I might find something so wrong that I have to make a radical change.
- If I find something wrong, I'll have to delay delivery.
- I'm a code writer, not a code tester.
- If I find something wrong, I'll lose plausible deniability unless I take the time to fix it.
- It's really elegant the way it is. I don't want to be bothered with special cases that no one's likely to hit anyway.
- Users are the best testers. They have real test cases.

It's a rare programmer who doesn't have at least one of those going on (our hands are up too). Unfortunately, as dirty as the job is, it's yours and no one else's responsibility to make sure you deliver the very best code you can. So let's wade past the discomfort and the apathy and see what we can do.

Testing is getting more attention these days, thanks to a new methodology called Extreme Programming (XP), which states not only that everything shall be tested, but also that the tests will be written before the code they test. Here's a breakdown of different types of testing:

- *Inspection testing, or code walkthroughs.* Nothing is executed; people simply read the code.
- *Unit testing.* Each individual component is tested for the expected response under the design conditions and for correct error responses under all other conditions.

  Although there is no clear definition of how large a component can be tested, it is expected that it is small enough so that you can test all or nearly all the possible boundary conditions and execution paths and it is relatively easy to test the component in isolation. In most languages, the unit is a subroutine.

- *Integration testing.* This is testing whether a subroutine or group of subroutines functions according to design specifications with regards to API and linked with whatever other subroutines exist in a project. Issues to consider at this stage are namespace conflicts and memory leaks.

- *System testing.* The entire system (or whatever you call the thing you are delivering) is tested against the customer's requirements. (You did get requirements from the customer, didn't you?)

- *Regression testing.* This is the same as system testing, but the term implies that it is performed whenever any changes have been made to the system to ensure that the system still performs correctly and has not *regressed* to some other state.

- *Saturation testing, or load testing.* In a system that handles arbitrary loads (such as Web servers) it's important to find out what its limits are. This type of testing throws more and more simultaneous requests at the system until it fails or you have exceeded the requirements by a vast margin.

- *Acceptance testing.* This one isn't for you; it's for the customer. They need a way to tell whether what you've delivered to them meets their requirements. In an ideal world, they write the test themselves, and warrant that it matches the requirements they gave you. Don't be surprised if they ask you to write the tests for them, though. (Don't be surprised if they ask, "What's acceptance testing?" either.)

Few projects include all these types of testing; the distinctions among several of them are blurred anyway, and it will usually be acceptable to leave some out. XP requires only unit testing and regression testing; code walkthroughs of a sort happen because programmers are required to work in pairs.

Let's go through each type of testing and see what it means to a Perl programmer.

6.1 Inspection Testing

Other people are going to look at your code—they may find bugs—and they are very likely to comment on its readability and maintainability. If you picked a consistent style (see Perl of Wisdom #6) and consistently commented your code, they should have fewer nits to pick in that department.

You are not bound to accept every comment from the people reviewing your code (people who should be your peers; this process is *not* a management function), only the ones that make sense. The more you can keep your ego in check, the better, because you want to be able to learn from the process; merely showing off how brilliant your code is won't do anything to improve your craft.

A mammoth bone of contention that often arises is the issue of code clarity. If a neophyte programmer presents code to veterans, the latter will suggest all sorts of optimizations to abbreviate the code. This issue is more acute with Perl than perhaps with any other language ever invented. Even more vexingly, an expert programmer showing code to novices will hear all kinds of standard idioms attacked as "obfuscated," "too clever," or "incomprehensible."

There is no universal solution to this problem. If the practice at your business is to code at the level of the lowest common denominator, then the presence of a beginner will drag the whole team down. If the practice is to code to the level of the majority then the value of an expert will be diminished by an average team. On the other hand, the expert's code will be useless to the company if no one who's left on the team can understand it after the expert leaves (although it might motivate some of them to improve their skills). Only a wise manager can decide what's right for their team. If you're managing a team that harbors a prima donna, try suggesting to that person that the greatest wizard of all is the one who can present an advanced idiom in a way that makes it understandable to novices.[1]

---

1. If they pooh-pooh this suggestion, refer them to the writings of physicist Richard Feynmann, who is probably one of their heroes, and who firmly believed that any physical principle that was truly understood could be explained at the high school level.

The one tip we can offer is to use standard idioms and styles wherever possible. If you code something in a way that is familiar to other people, then even if they don't work at your business they can be hired, or other team members can learn the idiom as it is shared through books and the Internet. If a reviewer says you've coded something for which a well-known idiom exists, find out what that idiom is. The benefit in this respect of frequenting Internet newsgroups and mailing lists is huge.

If you're creating large systems in Perl, they should almost certainly be broken down along object-oriented lines. It will be much easier to understand each object class one at a time.

You might also consider the CPAN module `B::Fathom`. This generates a score representing a measure of complexity of the code it is fed.

6.2 Unit Testing

Perl shines at unit testing. Although there's no empirical data to prove this, conversational evidence suggests that most Perl programs are short enough that unit testing is the same as system testing. People often report that their programs shrink by 90% when converted from C to Perl (our experience bears this out). A 1000-line C program requires more heavy-duty testing than a 100-line Perl program.

6.2.1 The One-Liner

Although not strictly in the category of unit testing, we must mention the utility of the one-liner. Several flags in Perl make it possible for you to test an idiom without even having to write a script, but instead just entering the code on the command line. The first of these is:

- `-e code`: Execute `code` as though it were in a script. Put single quotes around `code` on Unix to prevent the shell being confused by metacharacters, and use double quotes on DOS.

We can combine this with the −w flag if we want to enable warnings. Let's say that we want to check on which way printf rounds 0.5:

```
%  perl -we 'printf "%1.1f %1.f\n", $_+.5, $_+.5 for 1..4'
1.5 2
2.5 2
3.5 4
4.5 4
```

(No, that's not a mistake; that's the way the IEEE floating point standard says it should work.)

Note by the way that the −e flag has to be the last one before code; you can't type perl −ew ...

- −p, −n: Execute code for every line from the input, and either print $_ automatically when done (−p) or not (−n).

Say you want to find out the ASCII codes generated by certain keys on your keyboard; you could type

```
$ perl -pe 's/(.)/" ".ord $1/ge'
```

and then hit a key followed by a newline to see its ASCII value.

- −l (the letter 'ell', not the number one): Append an automatic newline to print statements. When combined with −n or −p, also automatically chomp the newline character off the input.

Let's say you want to find which users listed in a Unix /etc/passwd file have directories under /home:

```
%  perl -nle 's/:.*//; print if -d "/home/$_"' /etc/passwd
```

This can most usefully be used as a first stage in a pipeline of commands that then go on to do other things with its results. Or you might want a Perl program as the final stage of a pipeline that periodically reports how many lines it has read:

```
% ... | perl -nle 'BEGIN{ $SIG{ALRM} = \
                          sub{ print $.; alarm 10 }; \
                          alarm 10 }'
```

In this case, nothing at all is being executed in the loop for each line of input!

The -l flag is particularly useful in one-liners or in short test programs in which you have only a handful of print statements and want to save the trouble of typing \n in all of them. However, don't leave it in production code; setting a global flag like this affects the behavior of all print statements and will produce unpleasant results from using modules that don't expect it (such as CGI.pm and Benchmark).

- -M*module:* Perform a use *module* before executing any code.

You can use this to impose strictness on your one-liners, and also as a quick test to see if a module you want is installed:

```
% perl -MTime::HiRes -e 0
```

This prints nothing if the Time::HiRes module is installed but complains if it isn't.

- -c: This flag gives you the ability to check the syntax of a Perl program without actually running it. Because so much error checking is deferred until run-time in Perl, this is of limited use, but there are certainly times when it can save some time by serving as a quick sanity check.

23 **Use one-liners for rapid prototyping of small code constructs.**

Some Web shrines to the power of the one-liner have been erected at `http://history.perl.org/oneliners/` and `http://www.itknowledge.com/tpj/one-liners01.html` (one-liners that previously appeared in *The Perl Journal*).

6.2.2 Assert Yourself

The CPAN module `Carp::Assert`, by Michael G. Schwern, exports the routine `assert`, which allows you to trigger fatal exceptions with explanations during testing and then disable them globally before putting the application into use.

6.2.3 Design by Contract

Design by Contract is an idea from the Eiffel world that says you can add to your routines tests that express conditions that should be true before and after they execute, and conditions that should be true all the time. The new `Class::Contract` module by Damian Conway provides this facility for object-oriented modules, although you need to use its methods for creating your objects; it would be hard to retrofit to an existing class.

6.3 System or Regression Testing

Perl comes with code for testing perl itself, and you can use these same tools for your regression tests. They are deceptively simple. The `Test::Harness` module maintained by Andreas König exports a routine `runtests` that takes as arguments the names of programs to run. It looks for a header line of the form "1..*max*" and output lines that say either "`ok` *n*" or "`not ok` *n*", where *n* is between 1 and *max*; all other output is ignored and discarded. When it's done with all the tests, it prints a summary containing either the magic word "successful" or the dreaded word "FAILED."

But wait, there's more. The `Test` module[2] by Joshua Nathaniel Pritikin makes it easy for your programs to output the "ok/not ok" lines. It exports the routine `ok`, which evaluates its arguments to determine which kind of line to output (based on a whole slew of convenient possibilities depending on the number and type of arguments), and the subroutine `plan`, for outputting the header containing the number of tests.

Therefore `Test` provides assertion mechanisms for outputting success/failure information that can then be logged from multiple scripts by `Test::Harness`, which will output a summary telling you whether the entire test passed or identifying which subtests failed.

As if that weren't enough—these Perl people really are lazy[3]—Perl comes with yet more utilities to automate the construction of the test framework. The `h2xs` program creates a skeleton directory tree for a new Perl module (although in a pinch it could be adapted to an application instead), including a file `Makefile.PL` and a skeleton test script `test.pl`.

When you run this file through perl (which you typically need to modify somewhat to reflect additional files and dependencies that your module requires), it generates a much larger makefile (although a size that is typical for today's makefiles). That makefile includes a `test` target that runs `Test::Harness::runtests` over `test.pl`. If you create a subdirectory called `t` before you create the makefile, `make test` includes every file in that directory with a name ending in `.t` in the `runtests`.

Here's a quick example to show how all these things play together. Let's say that we're going to create a module that exports a function to convert the names of colors to their numerical values. On many Unix systems there is a conversion table in the file `rgb.txt`, often stored in `/usr/lib/X11`, so we'll just appropriate that for our use. Let's call this package `ColorConv`, so we start out with h2xs:

---

2. Both these modules are considerably more powerful than indicated in our brief explanations; we're just hitting the highlights.

3. Remember, that's a virtue.

```
% h2xs -XA -n ColorConv
Writing ColorConv/ColorConv.pm
Writing ColorConv/Makefile.PL
Writing ColorConv/test.pl
Writing ColorConv/Changes
Writing ColorConv/MANIFEST
```

Then we'll descend into the new directory ColorConv and start editing ColorConv.pm. You'll notice that it's already been populated with documentation stubs and a framework which we leave out of the following version in which we show just our code:

```perl
package ColorConv;
use strict;

my %COLOR;
if (open COLORS, '/usr/lib/X11/rgb.txt')
   {
   while (<COLORS>)
      {
      next unless my ($r, $g, $b, $name) =
          /^\s*(\d+)\s+(\d+)\s+(\d+)\s+(.*)/;
      $name =~ tr/ //d;
      $COLOR{lc $name} = sprintf "#%02X%02X%02X", $r, $g, $b;
      }
   close COLORS;
   }
   else
   {
   warn
     "Can't open color file ($!), translations impossible\n";
   }

sub conv
   {
   $COLOR{lc shift} || 'Unknown';
   }

1;
```

You'll notice there's also a `test.pl` created for you. Although it doesn't use `Test.pm` by default, we'll alter it so that it does:

```
#!/usr/bin/perl -w
use strict;
use ColorConv;
use Test;

my %color = (bisque  => '#FFE4C4',
     tomato1 => '#FF6347',
     red     => '#FF0000',
     green   => '#00FF00',
     blue    => '#0000FF',
     plum    => '#DDA0DD',
     puce    => 'Unknown');

plan tests => scalar keys %color;

for (keys %color)
   {
   ok(ColorConv::conv($_), $color{$_});
   }
```

Now when we run this, the output is as follows:

```
1..7
ok 1
ok 2
ok 3
ok 4
ok 5
ok 6
ok 7
```

And if we were to create the makefile right now (with `perl Makefile.PL`), that's what we'd see if we typed `make test`. However, if we create a subdirectory `t` first and put `test.pl` in `t/testcol.t` instead, we can get a higher level perspective with `Test::Harness` when we run `make test`:

```
% make test
```

```
PERL_DL_NONLAZY=1 /usr/bin/perl -Iblib/arch -Iblib/lib -I/usr/
lib/perl5/5.6.0/i586-linux -I/usr/lib/perl5/5.6.0 -e 'use
Test::Harness qw(&runtests $verbose); $verbose=0; runtests
@ARGV;' t/*.t
t/testcol...........ok
All tests successful.
```

In this case, `testcol.t` was the only `.t` file in the `t` directory. If we were to put more there, each of them would be run in turn, so we could build up a suite of regression tests.

How should you craft regression tests? A deceptively simple question. Jarkko Hietaniemi's advice is, "Try to break your own code. Give functions/ programs too few/many arguments, arguments of the wrong type (e.g., a directory when a file is expected). Give undef or empty or huge scalars, strings when numbers are expected, and vice versa. Think Evil." You'll notice we took that advice to heart when we added a test that the absent (unfairly, in our opinion) color puce caused the right kind of error. Your regression tests should exercise as many as possible of the failure modes your code can produce.

Perl itself runs approximately *12,000* tests using this framework when you type `make test`, so the capability can support large projects.

6.3.1 Coverage Analysis

At this point we might want to determine whether we're really testing all the code in our application or whether some is getting missed. The CPAN module `Devel::Coverage` by Randy J. Ray does just this. It's a debugger plugin that counts the number of times each executable line of code is visited.[4] You can then look for any that has a count of zero.

---

4. Since it can't distinguish among multiple statements on the same line, don't put multiple statements on the same line if one might be executed but not another.

Here's an example. (In practice, this tool would be most useful on much larger programs.) Here we've included our test data in the program itself to make it more self-contained.

```
1   #!/usr/bin/perl -wd:Coverage
2   use strict;
3
4   my (%scientific, %float, %integer);
5   while (<DATA>) {
6       chomp;
7       if (/(-?\d+\.\d?E[-+]?\d+)/i) {
8           $scientific{$1}++;
9       }
10      elsif (/(-?\d+\.\d?)/) {
11          $float{$1}++;
12      }
13      elsif (/(-?\d+)/) {
14          $integer{$1}++;
15      }
16  }
17
18  __END__
19  4
20  4.5
21  -3E3
22  5
23  6
24  3.2
```

When we run this program, it puts its output in a file with the same name but with .cvp appended. This is in a raw format that is converted to something appealing by running it through the coverperl program that comes with Devel::Coverage:

```
3       line 2
1       line 4
7       line 5
6       line 6
6       line 7
0       line 8
```

```
2      line 11
4      line 14
```

(Only the executable lines are listed.) We can quickly see that line 8 was never executed, and a quick check of our code shows that the regex didn't match the input data; either the regex or the data must be at odds with the requirements.

6.4 Saturation Testing

For string inputs, Perl can succinctly generate random strings of a given length:

```
{
my @visible = grep /[[:print:]]/, map chr, 0..255;
sub randstring { join '', map $visible[rand @visible],
                                 1 .. shift }
}
```

and the entire set of alphabetic strings of a given length:

```
sub permstring { 'a'x$_[0] .. 'z'x$_[0] }
```

although the memory required won't make this useful for a length of more than about five.[5] See also the CPAN module `String::Random`.

For simulating interactive sessions with users, you may want the CPAN module `Expect.pm` by Austin Schutz. It inherits its name from the popular Tcl tool called `expect`.

---

5. You could avoid the memory problem (in version 5.005 or later) by using the expression inside a `foreach` loop instead of a subroutine, but then you'd get clobbered by the amount of time to go through the loop. The finite nature of the universe has a way of catching up with you.

6.5 Acceptance Testing

You need a way to deliver your code to the customer, and the makefile we built earlier contains several targets for this purpose:

- `tardist`: Make a Unix tar file (converting files to Unix format if you're not on Unix).
- `dist`: Defaults to `$(DIST_DEFAULT)`, which in turn defaults to `tardist`.
- `uutardist`: Make a uuencoded tarfile (suitable for e-mailing).
- `zipdist`: Make a compressed distribution file with the program specified by `$(ZIP)`.

The full documentation for the makefile can be retrieved with `perldoc ExtUtils::MakeMaker`.

6.6 References

- *Improving Software Quality*, by Lowell Jay Arthur (Wiley & Sons, 1993)
- *Extreme Programming Explained*, by Kent Beck (Addison-Wesley, 1999)
- *Code Complete*, by Steve McConnell (Microsoft Press, 1993)
- *The Art of Software Testing*, by Glenford J. Meyers (Wiley & Sons, 1979)

The Perl Debugger

"My name is Ozymandius, King of Kings,
Look on my Works, ye Mighty, and despair!"
Ozymandius, *by Percy Bysshe Shelley*

An interactive, command-line-oriented debugger fails the practical definition of an instrument of torture, but this distinction appears too fine for many otherwise fearless, capable programmers who shiver and cringe with despair when asked to use one. Debuggers, while not inherently evil, do seem rather esoteric, and their use more an art form than a practical skill.

 I've had people in my classes who thought debuggers were tools to remove bugs from their code. If only this were so. Therefore it probably bears explaining that, contrary to its name, a debugger is merely a device that allows you to execute a program incrementally while having an opportunity to examine and change its internal state as it does so.

This concept is not new with Perl. Interactive debuggers like the one in Perl have been around for decades, and the only thing special about Perl's is the degree of access it gives you to its internals, allowing you to create a customized debugging interface if you wish (more on this later).

7.1 Basic Operation

Normally perl runs your program unhindered, but the debugger is a way of allowing both perl and you to run your program together. At any point in the execution of your program you can have perl pause and tell you what it has done so far. Think of the Perl run-time system as a mouse that gobbles up a trail of bread crumbs that are the opcodes of your program. The debugger allows you to tell the mouse to stop at points of your choosing and interrogate it as to the contents of its digestive system. And if you don't like the values of some of the variables, you can change them (we will not attempt to extend our metaphor to include this).

In fact, the debugger for Perl is a plugin written using hooks enabled by the −d flag. It's possible to write programs that do things with those hooks other than present an interactive command line-oriented interface, and several people have done so. We've already seen one example, `Devel::Coverage` in Chapter 6, and we'll visit `Devel::DProf` in Chapter 11.

7.2 Starting

The `-d` command line option makes your script run under the debugger. You can either add it to the options in the `#!` line at the beginning of your script, or you can override the options by explicitly running the script through perl. So for example, if `wombat.pl` currently has the `-w` option set, you can either change its first line to

```
#!/usr/bin/perl -wd
```

or you can type

```
% perl -wd wombat.pl
```

to debug it without having to change the script. Unlike some debuggers, with this one you supply arguments to the program on the command line, not as part of a debugger command; for example:

```
% perl -wd wombat.pl kangaroo platypus wallaby
```

The debugger will announce itself and provide a prompt:

```
Loading DB routines from perl5db.pl version 1.07
Emacs support available.

Enter h or `h h' for help.

main::(wombat.pl:1):    my $marsupial = shift;
  DB<1>
```

From now on we will elide everything before the first prompt (and the code on which it is stopped) when reproducing debugger sessions.

To begin, let's look at some simple commands. The very first of interest, of course, is h for help. The output from this is several screens long, which gives us an opportunity to mention an option we can apply to all commands: put a vertical bar (|) before any command and it will run the output through your pager (the program that prints things one screen at a time, waiting for you to tell it when to continue—more or less more or less).

7.2.1 Watch the Code Execute: *s, n, r*

Enter this simple program into debug.pl:

```
#!/usr/local/bin/perl -w
use strict;

my @parole = qw(Salutations Hello Hey);

print_line(@parole);
print "Done\n";

# Our subroutine accepts an array, then prints the
# value of each element appended to "Perl World."
sub print_line
    {
    my @parole = @_;
    foreach (@parole)
        {
        print "$_ Perl World\n";
        }
    }
```

Now run it under the debugger and step through the program one statement at a time using the n (next) command:

```
% perl -dw debug.pl
main::(debug.pl:4):      my @parole = qw(Salutations Hello Hey);
  DB<1> n
main::(debug.pl:6):      &print_line(@parole);
  DB<1> n
Salutations Perl World
```

```
Hello Perl World
Hey Perl World
main::(debug.pl:7):        print "Done\n";
  DB<1> n
Done
Debugged program terminated.  Use q to quit or R to restart, use
O inhibit_exit to avoid stopping after program termination, h
q, h R or h O to get additional info.
  DB<1> q
```

Before the prompt, the debugger prints the source line(s) containing the statement to be executed in the next step. (If you have more than one executable statement in a line, it prints the line each time you type n until it's done executing all the statements on the line.) Notice the output of our program going to the terminal is intermingled with the debugger text. Notice also when we called `print_line(@parole)`, we executed all the statements in the subroutine before we got another prompt.

(From now on, we won't reproduce the optimistic `Debugged program terminated` blurb printed by the debugger.)

Suppose we wanted to step through the code inside subroutines like `print_line`. That's the reason for s (single step). Let's see how it's used, along with another handy stepping command, r (return):

```
% perl -d debug.pl
main::(debug.pl:4):        my @parole = qw(Salutations Hello Hey);
  DB<1> n
main::(debug.pl:6):        print_line(@parole);
  DB<1> s
main::print_line(debug.pl:13):      my @parole = @_;
  DB<1> n
main::print_line(debug.pl:14):        foreach (@parole)
main::print_line(debug.pl:15):          {
  DB<1>
main::print_line(debug.pl:16):          print "$_ Perl World\n";
  DB<1> r
Salutations Perl World
Hello Perl World
```

```
Hey Perl World
void context return from main::print_line
main::(debug.pl:7):       print "Done\n";
  DB<1> s
Done
Debugged program terminated.
```

The effect of r is to execute all the code up to the end of the current subroutine. (All these command letters are copied from existing popular Unix command line debuggers and are mnemonic—next, step, return). In addition, note that just hitting carriage return as a command repeats the last n or s command (and if there hasn't been one yet, it does nothing).

7.2.2 Examining Variables: *p, x, V*

Stepping through code is dandy, but how do we check our variables' values? Use either p *expression* to print the result of the expression (which is equivalent to printing to the filehandle $DB::OUT, so *expression* is put in list context) or x *variable*, which prints a variable in a pleasantly formatted form, following references. Once again, with the simple program:

```
% perl -wd debug.pl
main::(debug.pl:4):       my @parole = qw(Salutations Hello Hey);
  DB<1> p @parole
  DB<2> n
main::(debug.pl:6):       print_line(@parole);
  DB<2> p @parole
SalutationsHelloHey
  DB<3> x @parole
0  'Salutations'
1  'Hello'
2  'Hey'
```

In the first command, we instruct the debugger to print the value of @parole. However, the @parole assignment has yet to execute, so nothing comes out. Step past the assignment and then print the value with p; we see the current state of the array in a list format. Print the array value with x, and we see the individual elements formatted with array indices (a pretty print).

This might look familiar if you've been playing with the `Data::Dumper` module we referenced in Chapter 5. In fact, the output of `x` is intentionally very similar.

You can see all of the *dynamic* variables in a given package (default: `main::`) with the `V` command. This isn't as useful as it sounds because, unlike the `x` or `p` commands, it won't show you any *lexical* variables (which you declared with `my`). Yet you want to make as many of your variables as possible lexical ones (see Perl of Wisdom #8). Unfortunately there is no (easy) way to dump out all the lexical variables in a package, so you're reduced to printing the ones you know about.

A common problem is running off the end of the program and getting the `Debugged program terminated` message. At that point, all your variables have been destroyed. If you want to inspect the state of variables after the last line of your program has executed, add a dummy line (a `1` by itself will work) so that you can set a breakpoint on it.

Tip: when examining a hash, examine a *reference* to it instead. This lets the `x` command see the datatype you're inspecting instead of being handed the list that it evaluates to, and it can format it more appealingly:

```
  DB<1> %h = (Craig   => 'Stirling', \
             Sharron => 'Macready', Richard => 'Barrett');
  DB<2> x %h
0  'Sharron'
1  'Macready'
2  'Craig'
3  'Stirling'
4  'Richard'
5  'Barrett'
  DB<3> x \%h
0  HASH(0x8330d5c)
   'Craig' => 'Stirling'
   'Richard' => 'Barrett'
   'Sharron' => 'Macready'
```

Examine references to hashes instead of the hashes themselves in the debugger to get well-formatted output.

7.2.3 Examining Source: *l, -, w, .*

Sometimes you want more of the context of your program than just the current line. The following commands show you parts of your source code:

l	List successive windows of source code starting from the current line about to be executed.
l x + y	List $y + 1$ lines of source starting from line x.
l x - y	List source lines x through y.
-	List successive windows of source code before the current line.
w	List a window of lines around the current line.
w *line*	List a window of lines around *line*.
.	Reset pointer for window listings to current line.

Source lines that are breakable (i.e., can have a breakpoint inserted before them—see the following section) have a colon after the line number.

7.2.4 Playing in the Sandbox

Since the debugger is a full-fledged Perl environment, you can type in Perl code on the fly to examine its effects under the debugger;[1] some people do this as a way of testing code quickly without having to enter it in a script or type in everything perfectly before hitting end-of-file. (You just saw us do this at the end of section 7.2.2.)

---

1. So, you might wonder, how would you enter Perl code which happened to look like a debugger command (because you'd defined a subroutine l, perhaps)? In versions of Perl prior to 5.6.0, if you enter leading white space before text, the debugger assumes it must be Perl code and not a debugger command. So be careful not to hit the space bar by accident before typing a debugger command. This was no longer true as of version 5.6.0.

Type `perl -de 0` to enter this environment.[2] Let's use this as a sandbox for testing Perl constructs:

```
% perl -de 0
DB<1> $_ = 'What_do*parens-in=split+do%again?';
  DB<2> @a = split /(\W+)/;
  DB<3> x @a
0   'What_do'
1   '*'
2   'parens'
3   '-'
4   'in'
5   '='
6   'split'
7   '+'
8   'do'
9   '%'
10   'again'
11   '?'
```

You can even use this feature to *change* the values of variables in a program you are debugging, which can be a legitimate strategy for seeing how your program behaves under different circumstances. If the way your program constructs the value of some internal variable is complex and it would require numerous changes in the input to have it form the variable differently, then a good way of playing "What if?" is to stop the program at the right place in the debugger and change the value by hand. How would we stop it? Let's see . . .

7.2.5 Breakpointing: *c, b, L*

An important feature of a debugger is the ability to allow your program to continue executing until some condition is met. The most common such condition is the arrival of the debugger at a particular line in your source. You can tell the Perl debugger to run until a particular line number with the `c` (for continue) command:

---

2. There are many expressions other than 0 that would work equally well, of course. Perl just needs something innocuous to run.

```
main::(debug.pl:4):      my @parole = qw(Salutations Hello Hey);
  DB<1> c 16
main::print_line(debug.pl:16):          print "$_ Perl World\n";
  DB<2>
```

What the debugger actually did was set a *one-time breakpoint* at line 16 and then executed your code until it got there. If it had hit another breakpoint earlier, it would have stopped there first.

So what's a breakpoint? It's a marker set by you immediately before a line of code, invisible to anyone but the perl debugger, which causes it to halt when it gets there and return control to you with a debugger prompt. If you have a breakpoint set at a line of code that gets printed out with one of the source examination commands listed earlier, you'll see a b next to it. It's analogous to putting a horse pill in the trail of bread crumbs the mouse follows so the mouse gets indigestion and stops to take a breather (we really have to give up this metaphor soon).

You set a breakpoint with the b command; the most useful forms are b *line* or b *subroutine* to set a breakpoint either at a given line number or immediately upon entering a subroutine. To run until the next breakpoint, type c. To delete a breakpoint, use d *line* to delete the breakpoint at line number *line* or D to delete all breakpoints.

In certain situations you won't want to break the next time you hit a particular breakpoint, but only when some condition is true, like every hundredth time through a loop. You can add a third argument to b specifying a condition that must be true before the debugger will stop at the breakpoint. For example,

```
main::(debug.pl:4):      my @parole = qw(Salutations Hello Hey);
  DB<1> l
4==>    my @parole = qw(Salutations Hello Hey);
5
6:      print_line(@parole);
7:      print "Done\n";
8
9       # Our subroutine which accepts an array, then prints
10      # the value of each element appended to "Perl World."
```

```
11        sub print_line
12            {
13:           my @parole = @_;
  DB<1> l
14:           foreach (@parole)
15                {
16:               print "$_ Perl World\n";
17                }
18            }
  DB<1> b 16 /Hey/
  DB<2> c
Salutations Perl World
Hello Perl World
main::print_line(debug.pl:16):          print "$_ Perl World\n";
  DB<2> p
Hey
```

Notice that we've demonstrated several things here: the source listing command l, the conditional breakpoint with the criterion that $_ must match /Hey/, and that $_ is the default variable for the p command (because p just calls print).

The capability of the debugger to insert code that gets executed in the context of the program being debugged does not exist in compiled languages and is a significant example of the kind of thing that is possible in a language as well designed as Perl.

The command L lists all breakpoints.

7.2.6 Taking Action: *a, A*

An even more advanced use of the facility to execute arbitrary code in the debugger is the *action* capability. With the a command (syntax: a *line code*), you can specify code to be executed just before a line would be executed. (If a breakpoint is set for that line, the action executes first; then you get the debugger prompt.) The action can be arbitrarily complicated and, unlike this facility in debuggers for compiled languages, lets you reach into the program itself:

```
main::(debug.pl:4):      my @parole = qw(Salutations Hello Hey);
  DB<1> a 16 s/Hey/Greetings/
  DB<2> c
Salutations Perl World
Hello Perl World
Greetings Perl World
Done
Debugged program terminated.
```

L also lists any actions you have created. Delete all the installed actions
with the A command. This process is commonly used to insert tracing code on
the fly. For example, suppose you have a program executing a loop containing
way too much code to step through, but you want to monitor the state of certain
variables each time it goes around the loop. You might want to confirm what's
actually being ordered in a shopping cart application test (looking at just a
fragment of an imaginary such application here):

```
  DB<1> l 79-91
79:     while (my $item = shift @shopping_basket)
80          {
81:         if ($item->in_stock)
82              {
83:             $inventory->remove($item);
84:             $order->add($item);
85              }
86          else
87              {
88:             $order->back_order($item);
89:             $inventory->order($item);
90              }
91          }
  DB<2> a 81 printf "Item: %25s, Cost: %5.2f\n",
  $item->name, $item->cost
  DB<3> c 92
Item:           Forbidden Planet, Cost: 24.50
Item:        Kentucky Fried Movie, Cost: 29.95
Item:                  Eraserhead, Cost: 14.75
main::(cart.pl:92):     $customer->charge($order->total);
  DB<3>
```

7.2.7 Watch It: *W*

Suppose you want to break on a condition that is dictated not by a particular
line of code but by a change in a particular variable. This is called a *watch-
point*, and in Perl you set it with the `W` command followed by the name of a
variable.[3]

Let's say you're reading a file of telephone numbers and to whom they belong
into a hash, and you want to stop once you've read in the number 555-1212 to
inspect the next input line before going on to check other things:

```
main::(foo:1):  my %phone;
  DB<1> l 1-5
1==>      my %phone;
2:        while (<>) {
3:          my ($k, $v) = split;
4:          $phone{$k} = $v;
5         }
  DB<2> W $phone{'555-1212'}
  DB<3> c
Watchpoint 0:    $phone{'555-1212'} changed:
    old value:   undef
    new value:   'Information'
main::(foo:2):  while (<>) {
  DB<3> n
main::(foo:3):    my ($k, $v) = split;
  DB<3> p
555-1234 Weather
```

Delete all watchpoints with a blank `W` command.

---

3. In fact, Perl can monitor anything that evaluates to an lvalue, so you can watch just specific array or
   hash entries, for example.

7.2.8 Trace: *t*

The debugger's t command provides a trace mode for those instances that require a complete trace of program execution. Running the program with an active trace mode:

```
% perl -wd debug.pl
main::(debug.pl:4):       my @parole = qw(Salutations Hello Hey);
  DB<1> t
Trace = on
  DB<1> n
main::(debug.pl:6):       print_line(@parole);
  DB<1> n
main::print_line(debug.pl:13):      my @parole = @_;
main::print_line(debug.pl:14):      foreach (@parole)
main::print_line(debug.pl:15):         {
main::print_line(debug.pl:16):           print "$_ Perl World\n";
Salutations Perl World
main::print_line(debug.pl:14):      foreach (@parole)
main::print_line(debug.pl:15):         {
main::print_line(debug.pl:16):           print "$_ Perl World\n";
Hello Perl World
main::print_line(debug.pl:14):      foreach (@parole)
main::print_line(debug.pl:15):         {
main::print_line(debug.pl:16):           print "$_ Perl World\n";
Hey Perl World
main::print_line(debug.pl:14):      foreach (@parole)
main::print_line(debug.pl:15):         {
main::(debug.pl:7):     print "Done\n";
```

Notice that trace mode causes the debugger to output the call tree when execution enters the print_line subroutine.

7.2.9 Programmatic Interaction with the Debugger

You can put code in your program to force a call to the debugger at a particular point. For instance, suppose you're processing a long input file line by line and you want to start tracing when it reaches a particular line. You could set a conditional breakpoint, but you could also extend the semantics of your input by creating "enable debugger" lines. Consider the following:

```
while (<INPUT>)
  {
  $DB::trace = 1, next if /debug/;
  $DB::trace = 0, next if /nodebug/;
  # more code
  }
```

When run under the debugger, this enables tracing when the loop encounters an input line containing "debug" and ceases tracing upon reading one containing "nodebug". You can even force the debugger to breakpoint by setting the variable $DB::single to 1, which also happens to provide a way you can debug code in BEGIN blocks (which otherwise are executed before control is given to the debugger).

7.2.10 Optimization

Although the Perl debugger displays lines of code as it runs, it's important to note that these are not what actually executes. Perl internally executes its compiled opcode tree, which doesn't always have a contiguous mapping to the lines of code you typed, due to the processes of compilation and optimization. If you have used interactive debuggers on C code in the past, you may be familiar with this process.

When debugging C programs on VAX/VMS, it was common for me to want to examine an important variable only to get the message that the variable was not in memory and had been "optimized away."

Perl has an optimizer to do as good a job as it can—in the short amount of time people will wait for compilation—of taking shortcuts in the code you've given it. For instance, in a process called *constant folding*, it does things like build a single string in places where you concatenate various constant strings together so that the concatenation operator need not be called at run-time.

The optimization process also means that perl may execute opcodes in an order different from the order of statements in your program, and therefore when the debugger displays the current statement, you may see it jump around oddly. As recently as version 5.004_04 of perl, this could be observed in a program like the following:

```
1    my @a = qw(one two three);
2    while ($_ = pop @a)
3        {
4        print "$_\n";
5        }
6    1;
```

See what happens when we step through this, again using perl 5.005_04 or earlier:

```
main::(while.pl:1):    my @a = qw(one two three);
  DB<1> n
main::(while.pl:6):    1;
  DB<1>
main::(while.pl:4):     print "$_\n";
  DB<1>
three
main::(while.pl:2):    while ($_ = pop @a)
  DB<1>
main::(while.pl:4):     print "$_\n";
  DB<1>
two
```

In fact, if we set a breakpoint for line 6 and ran to it, we'd get there before the loop executed at all. So it's important to realize that under some circumstances, what the debugger tells you about where you are can be confusing. If this inconveniences you, upgrade.

7.2.11 Another "Gotcha"

If you set a lexical variable as the last statement of a block, there is no way to see what it was set to if the block exits to a scope that doesn't include the lexical. Why would code do that? In a word, *closures*. For example,

```
{                       # Start a closure-enclosing block
my $spam_type;          # This lexical will outlive its block
sub type_spam
   {
   # ...
   $spam_type = $spam_types[complex_func()];
   }
}
```

In this case, either `type_spam` or some other subroutine in the closure block would have a good reason for seeing the last value of `$spam_type`. But if you're stepping through in the debugger, you won't see the value it gets set to on the last line because, after the statement executes, the debugger pops out to a scope where `$spam_type` is not in scope (unless `type_spam()` was called from within the enclosing block). Unfortunately, in this case, if the result of the function is not used by the caller, you're out of luck.

7.3 Getting Graphical

Programmers can choose from several graphical interfaces to the Perl debugger. We'll describe two of the free alternatives.[4] We won't provide much detail describing their use since they are simply graphical layers on top of Perl's internal debugger; all you need to do is find the buttons corresponding to the commands just described.

_____

4. There are a number of commercial (i.e., not free) products offering GUI Perl debugger interfaces and other IDE functionality. We omitted them merely because we didn't want to appear biased toward or against any particular vendor by inadvertently leaving one out.

7.3.1 ddd

ddd, developed by Andreas Zeller, is a GNU graphical interface to many debuggers, including Perl's; obtain it from http://www.gnu.org/software/ddd/ddd.html. No Windows port currently exists, but it builds easily enough on Linux when you download the requisite RPMs or package files. In Figure 7-1, note the breakpoint, current statement pointer, and various displays.

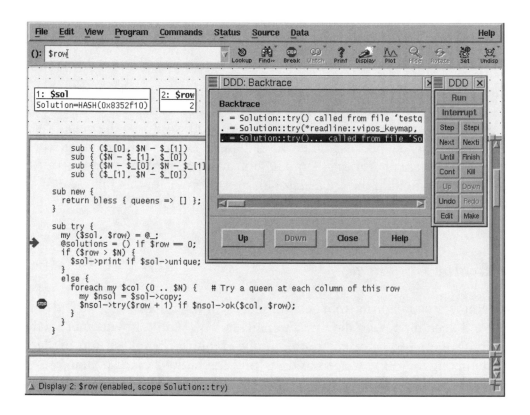

FIGURE 7-1. ddd used as an interface to the Perl debugger

(The application is an object-oriented program for solving the "*N* Queens" problem: Print out all the possible ways of placing *n* queens on an $n \times n$ chessboard so that no one is attacked by another.)

7.3.2 ptkdb

ptkdb, developed by Andrew E. Page, is a free, Tk-based, graphical interface to the built-in perl debugger, with a clean and intuitive design. Obtain ptkdb from `http://search.cpan.org/search?dist=Devel-ptkdb`. It also requires PerlTk by Nick Ing-Simmons (`http://search.cpan.org/search?dist=Bundle-Tk`).

ptkdb is invoked as a debugger plugin, so to debug myprog.pl, type

```
perl -d:ptkdb myprog.pl
```

There is little we need to add to the description of ptkdb. In Figure 7-2, we see that the current line is highlighted, nonbreakable line numbers are struck through, and the tabbed panes on the right are for inspecting expressions, subroutines, and breakpoints. The appearance of the interface can be extensively customized.

One key advantage of ptkdb is that it can be used to debug a Perl program used in a CGI process. We give examples of this in Chapter 13.

7.3.3 Emacs

More than a command line, less than a GUI, the free and insanely powerful GNU text editor includes quasi-graphical support for a simple but intuitive interface to the perl debugger via the cperl mode (see Chapter 3). To start a debug session in the active buffer, enter M-x perldb RET, and you'll get something like Figure 7-3, where one subwindow contains the source code, and the other is for interactions with the debugger.

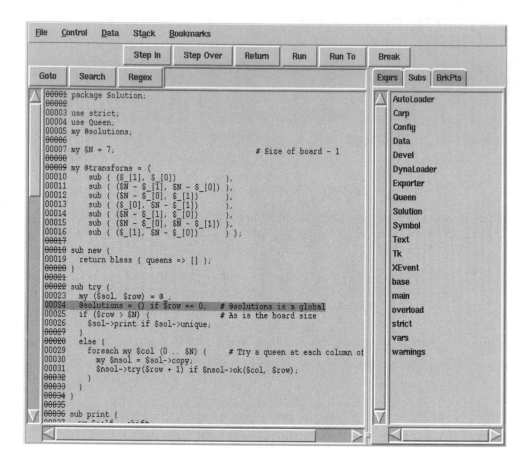

```
 File   Control   Data   Stack   Bookmarks

              Step In     Step Over    Return    Run    Run To    Break

   Goto     Search      Regex                                  Exprs  Subs  BrkPts

 00001 package Solution;                                        AutoLoader
 00002                                                          Carp
 00003 use strict;                                              Config
 00004 use Queen;                                               Data
 00005 my @solutions;                                           Devel
 00006                                                          DynaLoader
 00007 my $N = 7;                         # Size of board - 1   Exporter
 00008                                                          Queen
 00009 my @transforms = (                                       Solution
 00010      sub { ($_[1], $_[0])        },                      Symbol
 00011      sub { ($N - $_[1], $N - $_[0]) },                   Text
 00012      sub { ($N - $_[0], $_[1])   },                      Tk
 00013      sub { ($_[0], $N - $_[1])   },                      XEvent
 00014      sub { ($N - $_[1], $_[0])   },                      base
 00015      sub { ($N - $_[0], $N - $_[1]) },                   main
 00016      sub { ($_[1], $N - $_[0])   } );                    overload
 00017                                                          strict
 00018 sub new {                                                vars
 00019    return bless { queens => [] };                        warnings
 00020 }
 00021
 00022 sub try {
 00023    my ($sol, $row) = @_;
 00024    @solutions = () if $row == 0;   # @solutions is a global
 00025    if ($row > $N) {                # As is the board size
 00026      $sol->print if $sol->unique;
 00027    }
 00028    else {
 00029      foreach my $col (0 .. $N) {     # Try a queen at each column of
 00030        my $nsol = $sol->copy;
 00031        $nsol->try($row + 1) if $nsol->ok($col, $row);
 00032      }
 00033    }
 00034 }
 00035
 00036 sub print {
```

FIGURE 7-2. **The ptkdb interface**

The syntax highlighting is evident in the source code when viewed in color.
(Keywords in blue, subroutine prototypes in heavy blue, comments in red, and
double-quoted strings in gray; if you don't like any of those assignments, they
are easy to change.)

FIGURE 7-3. The emacs interface to the Perl debugger via `cperl-mode`

Emacs is available with any Linux system and can be downloaded for virtually any platform from `http://www.gnu.org/software/emacs/emacs.html`.

Don't overlook the use of debuggers as a teaching tool. I often use `ptkdb` to monitor the evolution of a variable (scalar, array, hash) as a program executes. Such a demonstration allows a new programer to observe a variable's value and scope in various situations—which is quite useful when you are forced to explain the difference between lexical variables and package variables.

Chapter 8

Syntax Errors

"Fire bad!"

Frankenstein's monster in a fit of homicidal frustration

"Typos bad!"

The first programmer, same emotion

We realize we're tempting scorn by devoting a chapter to a subject as prosaic as typos, but someone must do these dirty jobs. Why? Consider this extract from a shift.com article by Clive Thompson:[1]

> Still, by any standard, speed kills quality. Consider the research currently being conducted by Watts Humphrey, a 45-year veteran of the industry and a fellow of the Software Engineering Institute. By studying programmers as they work, he has found that they make one mistake for every seven to ten lines of code—a stunning level of errors. And almost one-fifth of those errors are simply typos. All in all, coders introduce bugs at the rate of 4.2 defects per hour of programming. If you crack the whip and force people to move more quickly, Humphreys notes, things get even worse. "[The industry] can't survive with this level of quality," he adds.

As long as we're being prosaic, let's go all the way and define a typo. *The American Heritage Dictionary* (third edition) merely states, "A typographical error" (which is accurate but just a bit too prosaic for our liking). So we'll just say that you've made a typo when the characters that come out on the screen are not the ones that you intended to type.

A program containing a typo can still be correct syntactically, even if not semantically, as the legions of typists who rely on the squiggly lines under spelling errors in Microsoft Word have discovered to their chagrin.[2]

Syntax simply refers to whether the program obeys the grammar the parser expects; *semantics* refers to what the program means. A move in a game of chess could be syntactically invalid (such as moving a pawn forward six

---

1. http://www.shift.com/shiftstd/SiteMap/frames/mag7.6.asp
   ?searchfor=7.6bombsquad
2. And don't expect the squiggly lines made under a clause it considers grammatically incorrect to save
   you either: Word 97 has no problem with the sentence, "Aye fought eyesore a putty cat."

spaces), or syntactically valid but semantically stupid (such as a castling that puts you a move away from being checkmated).

8.1 Typo Pathologies

Later we'll tackle the more complex issues of errors committed when you typed exactly what you intended to type, but the program still fails to work. This chapter discusses the humble typo: if you could see it, you'd know it was a mistake, and how to fix it.

The trick is to find the typo in the first place. We will unfurl an array of techniques for zeroing in on the miscreant. Fortunately, the scope of the typo is not unlimited; seldom does someone type a word entirely different from the one they were thinking of, for instance. The following quote from the Cambridge doctoral thesis of Stephen Moss appositely states the possible choices, although he was referring to the effect of channel errors on textual transmission:

1. *Deletion:* "The Prime Minister spent the weekend in the country shooting peasants."

2. *Insertion:* "The walkway across the trout hatchery was supported on concrete breams."

3. *Alteration:* "Say it with glowers"; "For sale: Volvo 144 with overdrive, fuel infection, etc."

4. *Transposition:* "Yet, down the road, you will still find the corner shop where the lady behind the counter will lovingly warp your presents."

Let's consider examples of each category of typo, and we'll show the strategy we followed to hunt them down and destroy them.

8.1.1 Deletion

The most common example of deletion must be the failure to place a semicolon between two statements. (Perl requires semicolons as statement separators, not statement terminators; the difference is that the last statement in a block does not require a trailing semicolon. We present this piece of wisdom to help you understand programs you may inherit that were written by people obsessed with minimizing typing: we recommend that you insert a semicolon after every statement, even at the end of a block, since you never know when you might come back later and insert another statement after it.)

```
$message = "Hello World";
print "$message\n"
exit;
```

Perl responds with

```
syntax error at line 3, next token "exit"
```

The Perl compiler, like every other compiler we know, often goes somewhat further in your program than the actual error before reporting a problem. Since we've never met a compiler that indicated an error for a line number *preceding* the first one containing an error, we can use Perl's report of the line number as an upper bound and work backwards from it.

 The actual syntax error in your program could occur not just on the line reported by Perl, but on any line preceding it.

In this case, the line it reported was the last line of the file anyway (which often happens), but them's the breaks.

The strategy for fixing this problem: "syntax error" tells you that Perl has determined the problem to be a straightforward typo (count your blessings), so you know what you're looking for—something that doesn't look like valid Perl, on or before line 3. Perl gives us an additional piece of information, that the next token is `exit`. If we're lucky, that means that the error occurred immediately before that word, so that's where we start looking. Immediately, we notice a missing semicolon on line 2.

Success! Problem located and identified. Case closed. (No, there's no substitute for looking over the code with a Mark I eyeball. However, if you have reams of code to search, you can reduce the amount you have to check by removing or commenting out parts of it selectively until you see the error message change.)

Now let's consider another missing semicolon that's far more insidious:

```
use strict
my $message = "Hello World\n";
print $message;
exit;
```

This program compiles fine; it even runs without error. Unfortunately, it also runs without output. What happened to the contents of $message? A long or a short way can be used to debug this problem. Let's try the long way first (the reason for this choice will become apparent in due course).

We'll fire up the debugger (see Chapter 7). The first (meaningful) output from the debugger is

```
main::(-:3):    print $message;
DB<1>
```

Hmm. Something's wrong here. The debugger halted at the first executable line of code. (A use statement is a compile time directive, so we don't expect to see that in the debugger.) Why aren't we seeing the assignment to $message? No wonder when we examine $message there's nothing there:

```
DB<1> x $message
 0  undef
```

For some reason, line 2 isn't considered executable. It isn't commented out, so it must be being executed at compile time instead. Hmm again. That rings a bell. Wait a minute, it comes right after a `use` statement. Could it be that Perl is considering it to be part of the `use` statement?

At this point, we discover the missing semicolon and probably are too relieved to care about why it happened. But for the curious among you, here's an explanation: the absence of the semicolon and the fact that all white space (including newlines) looks the same to Perl means that lines 1 and 2 parse as

```
use strict my $message = "Hello World\n";
```

If we look at the specification for the `use` statement, we see that it is

`use` Module *LIST*

So the name of the module can be followed by a list—and an assignment is a valid member of a list! Because evaluation occurs in the scope of the `use` statement, `my $message = "Hello Perl World\n";` ends up scoped inside the implicit `BEGIN` block created by `use`, and hence disappears by the next line because it was a lexical variable.

The debugger demonstration shows the long way to find our typo, but in this case a shorter error analysis method exists. The `-w` flag produces warnings for the more common Perl programming problems. Run the program with the `-w` flag and Perl returns

```
Name "main::message" used only once: possible typo at typo.pl
line 3.
Use of uninitialized value at typo.pl line 3.
```

As we now know, the assignment of `$message` happens in the wrong place due to the typo. The warning alerts us to the fact that when `$message` *is* used, it doesn't yet contain a defined value.

This example should trouble you. If you put `use strict` in all your programs (and if you aren't doing so already, you will by the time you finish this book), you should be wondering now whether the strictness is in effect. To check, remove my from the $message assignment. If strictness is in effect, Perl will complain that $message lacks an explicit package name.

```
use strict
$message = "Hello World";
print "$message\n";
exit;
```

On running, Perl returns: Hello World. Surprise! The typo prevents strictness from becoming enabled. The absence of the my keyword allows the assignment to succeed. (Since it's global, the fact that the assignment happens in an invisible BEGIN block doesn't matter.)

This is one of the most insidious errors conceivable: a single character mistake that causes no warning and no error yet prevents the very error checking the programmer was trying to enable.

8.1.2 A Puzzle

Here's another example of deletion. Can you figure out what's wrong?

```
use strict;
sub foo
   {
   my $sref = shift;
   foreach my $d (@)
      {
      find ($sref, $d);
      }
   }

sub find { }
```

The result:

```
Global symbol "$d" requires explicit package name at typo.pl
line 6.
syntax error at typo.pl line 7, near "}"
```

```
syntax error at typo.pl line 8, near "}"
Execution of typo.pl aborted due to compilation errors.
```

`foreach my $d (@)` should instead be `foreach my $d (@_)`. Well, `@)` is a valid variable in Perl—a strange variable to be sure, and not the kind of thing you want to be using intentionally—but a variable nevertheless. This robbed the `foreach` list of its closing parenthesis and caused a wonderful cascade of nonsense.

8.1.3 Insertion

Insertion typos probably occur as often as deletion typos, though with different pathologies. An additional character in a variable name is flagged by Perl (if you used `-w`), and a misspelled command generates a run-time exception. An insertion typo becomes dangerous when the typo is still a valid Perl statement but executes an unexpected function.

Consider a program with one extraneous character:

```
use strict;
my $x = 1;
my $y = 2;
$x == $y;
print "$x,$y\n";
```

Run the program and Perl prints: `1,2`. No errors or warnings are given; this is expected, since each program statement is valid Perl. Now consider a program that differs from the previous one by one character:

```
use strict;
my $x = 1;
my $y = 2;
$x = $y;
print "$x,$y\n";
```

When run, Perl prints: `2,2`. Output from the second program shows the value of `$x` set to the value of `$y`, whereas the first performs no such operation. What did the first program do? In line 4, $x=$y was intended, but $x==$y was coded. The former is an assignment to modify $x, the latter a Boolean test that modifies neither $x nor $y—a particularly nasty problem as both commands are correct Perl syntax, and both execute without a complaint, with or without use strict.

All this is very elementary, of course, until you wonder "What if I use -w?" Run our first program with -w and Perl returns:

```
Useless use of numeric eq in a void context.
File 'typo1.pl'; Line 4.
```

This reveals yet another reason to use -w in every program: with it, Perl can warn us that while our mistake resulted in syntactically valid Perl, it was odd Perl. It can't raise a red flag stating "An extra = on line 4!" but it can point out that we've executed an essentially useless operation.

8.1.4 Alteration

Let's examine another single typo program:

```
use strict;
$message = "Hello World';
print "$message\n";
exit;
```

On running, Perl returns the following:

```
Scalar found where operator expected at typo.pl line 3, at end
of line (Might be a runaway multi-line "" string starting on
line 2) (Do you need to predeclare print?)
syntax error at typo.pl line 3, near "print "$message "
Global symbol "message" requires explicit package name at
typo.pl line 3.
Backslash found where operator expected at typo.pl line 3, near
"$message \" (Missing operator before \?)
Bareword "n" not allowed while "strict subs" in use at typo.pl
line 3.
```

```
String found where operator expected at typo.pl line 3, at end
of line (Missing semicolon on previous line?)
Can't find string terminator '"' anywhere before EOF at typo.pl
line 3.
```

Seven error messages from one typo! Let's concentrate on the first error and ignore the rest for now. The first error complains about a scalar on line 3 instead of a typo. Luckily, we get a hint about the error:

```
Might be a runaway multi-line "" string starting on line 2
```

This suggests paying special attention to the use of quote marks on line 2, where we find the string delimited by a double quote (") and a single quote ('). String delimiters must match at the beginning and end. Since there are no interpolated variables or digraphs in this string, either kind of quote will work, as long as we use the same one at each end of the string.

 Handle only the first warning or error message output by Perl; don't bother reading the others, just recompile.

Error messages after the first one may be a cascade effect and therefore may be eliminated by removing the cause of the first message. It's usually not worth the time to analyze each message to determine whether this is the case.

8.1.5 Transposition

Regular expressions provide a fertile breeding ground for typos. Suppose you want to match and save the last string of letters preceded by white space on a line:

```
/\s([a-z])+$/i
```

Looks right, eh? Try it on an example, though:

```
while (<DATA>)
   {
```

```
    print "Match = $1\n" if /\s([a-z])+$/i;
    }
__END__
The boy stood on the burning duck
```

What comes out but

```
Match = k
```

Oops. We wanted the last word, not the last letter. Here's an approach to debugging this problem: We printed $1, which is the text saved between parentheses. We can ignore whatever else the regex contains and focus on what's between the parens, i.e., [a-z], which we immediately recognize as a character class that hasn't been qualified with a quantifier. Therefore it can represent only one character, which is what we got. (When saving parentheses match more than once in a regex because of a quantifier, only the last match gets saved. One might wish for a switch that would return all the matches in a list.)

As with most typos, identifying it is 90% of the goal. The fix is easy to predict: /\s([a-z]+)$/i.

Here's a higher-level sort of transposition. Can you tell what it is before reading the explanation?

```
#!/usr/bin/perl -w
use strict;

my $fmt = "%10s "x5;
printf "$fmt\n", qw(Kelvin Celsius Rankine
                    Fahrenheit Reaumur);
$fmt = "%10.2f "x5;
for (my $kelvin = 0; $kelvin += 10; $kelvin < 500)
    {
    my $celsius    = $kelvin - 273.15;
    my $rankine    = $kelvin * 9 / 5;
    my $fahrenheit = $rankine - 459.67;
    my $reaumur    = $celsius * 4 / 5;
```

```
    printf "$fmt\n",$kelvin,$celsius,$rankine,$fahrenheit,
$reaumur;
    }
```

Run this, and it does not terminate! You will be calculating temperatures beyond those experienced in the Big Bang. But the very first line of output is

```
Useless use of numeric lt (<) in void context at temp.pl line
13.
```

Weird. Line 13 is the `printf` statement, and it has no <. According to Perl of Wisdom #24, we should start scanning backwards until we find one. There it is at the beginning of the `for` statement: forgivably, we transposed the test and iterative clauses.

If you'd like to know why Perl fingered line 13 and not line 7 (the `for` statement), you'll find an explanation in Chapter 10.

8.2 A Menagerie of Typos

At this point, we're going to go on a tour of typo examples with different diagnoses.

8.2.1 Quotable Quotes

Our first program sets up a hash `%quotation` indexed by author and then goes on:

```
while (my ($author, $quote) = each %quotation)
    {
    print 'Quote of the Day: "$quote" by $author\n';
    }
```

This runs, but takes us too literally:

```
Quote of the Day: "$quote" by $author\nQuote of the Day:
"$quote" by $author\nQuote of the Day: "$quote" by $author\n...
```

Aha! Nothing is being interpolated because we're using single quotes. We change them to double quotes:

```
3   while (my ($author, $quote) = each %quotation)
4     {
5       print "Quote of the Day: "$quote" by $author\n";
6     }
```

Yikes, now we get three errors:

```
Scalar found where operator expected at typo.pl line 4, near
""Quote of the Day: "$quote"
        (Missing operator before $quote?)
syntax error at typo.pl line 4, near ""Quote of the Day:
"$quote"
String found where operator expected at typo.pl line 4, near
"$quote" by $author\n""
        (Missing operator before " by $author\n"?)
Execution of typo.pl aborted due to compilation errors.
```

Once again, we consider only the first message. Whenever Perl provides a hint after the error, read it carefully. Perl suggests that we omitted an operator before $quote, but why would it expect an operator in the middle of a string? Aha—we must not be in a string any more.

 At this point I would have pointed out that the syntax coloring feature of Emacs cperl mode would have shown this, but I promised Ed not to make fractious text editor advertisements.

At least we don't have to look far to find the problem; the string ended prematurely one character before $quote. There is, of course, more than one way to fix it. We could escape the " inside the string with backslashes, or we could use the spiffy qq operator, which allows us to pick any delimiter to use for a double-quoted string:

```
while (my ($author, $quote) = each %quotation)
   {
   print qq(Quote of the Day: "$quote" by $author\n);
   }
```

8.2.2 A Capital Typo

Our next horror feature is The Program That Wouldn't Die:

```
#!/usr/bin/perl
use Getopt::Std;

sub usage
  {
  print
     "Allowable options: -a, -c, -e, -n count, -u\n";
  Exit;
  }

usage() unless getopts('acen:u');
print "Starting program $0\n";
```

Let's run it:

```
% typo.pl -q
Unknown option: q
Allowable options: -a, -c, -e, -n count, -u
Starting program typo.pl
```

Why did this program keep going even after it went into the usage error routine? For the answer, this is the last time we're going to tell you:

Put use strict and -w in all your programs!

Because when we do, we see:

```
Bareword "Exit" not allowed while "strict subs" in use at
typo.pl line 8.
Execution of typo.pl aborted due to compilation errors.
```

We should have used `exit` instead of `Exit`. (Perl built-in functions do not contain capital letters, and the reserved words that do are all uppercase.) Better yet, we should have called `die` instead of `print`.

## Chapter 9

Run-time Exceptions

"When you have eliminated the impossible,
that which remains, however improbable, must be the truth."

Sherlock Holmes in A Study in Scarlet, *by Sir Arthur Conan Doyle*

I remember when I was writing my first program in an independently-compiled language (Fortran; before that I was just using interpreted BASIC). After much work, I got the program to compile without any errors. In glee, I turned to a co-worker and said, "All right! I'm done now!" A grin came over his face, and he said, "I doubt it." What awaited me at that point was the evil *run-time error*.

Perl is no slouch in the run-time error reporting department, and in fact, many errors that would occur at compile time in other languages happen at run time in Perl. For example, using a string in a numeric context: a strongly typed language would spot at compile time the attempt to assign a string to a numeric variable, but in Perl a scalar can switch between a string and a number according to whim.

We present here our bug-hunting approach to resolving run-time exceptions. There's no way to know whether you've gotten rid of all possible run-time bugs without running your program under every conceivable set of inputs and environmental changes that might possibly affect it.[1]

The most basic run-time error is that the program refuses to execute at all. If you've been checking your program's syntax with Perl's -c switch, you might have a program that has no syntax errors but gives you the error "Permission denied" when you run it. This just means that you're running on Unix and have not yet set the execute permission for your program. You might also get "Command not found" even though you can see the program is there! Relax; this just means you have a typo in the first line of your program (the #! or "shebang" line), and it's saying it can't find the program you've put there. Perhaps you typed `prel` instead of `perl` again (or left out the space before the -w flag, which this author just did). While we're at it, you might also get an error looking like `.nrecognized switch: -`, which can drive you crazy until you

---

1. Aside from proofs-of-correctness; but there again, proofs-of-correctness never seem to be attached to anything longer than 10 lines anyway.

discover that it's from running a program with DOS-style line terminations on Unix. Remove the ^Ms with a tool like `dos2unix` or `perl -pi.bak -e 's/\cM$//'`.

The distinction between an *error* and an *exception* may have been hitherto glossed over in this book, but at this point we need to make it clear. An *error* simply means that something went wrong; for instance, a system routine may return a value indicating that it can't do what you have asked. A good program institutes some error handling at this point and checks the return code (more on this later). But the program is still running.

An *exception* occurs (is "thrown," in the lingo) when some code declares that something intolerable has happened and Perl is simply not going to allow your program to continue running unless you specifically know how to handle (or "catch") the exception. At this point, your program could be in the middle of some arbitrarily deep nesting of subroutine calls and { } blocks. It ceases executing wherever it is, and starts to percolate back up this stack looking at each level for anything declared that could catch this exception. If it gets all the way to the top without finding such a handler, it executes a default exception handler, which in Perl's case means printing a message with `die` and exiting.

Run-time exceptions from Perl may be built in, caused by `use strict`, or generated by you. The `-w` flag can cause a run-time warning message to be displayed, but your program will continue executing. If you've followed good coding practices, you should be worried about this possibility, since it may indicate that Perl is working with bad data (data that should be defined but isn't). If you want to make sure Perl halts when such a warning is generated, you can put this pseudo signal handler near the beginning of your program:[2]

```
local $SIG{__WARN__} = sub { die $_[0] }
```

and Perl exits after printing the warning.

---

2. This is one of the few times where the difference between `warn` and `print STDERR` becomes apparent; the former is trapped by this sort-of signal handler, the latter is not.

9.1 Symbolic References

Now that you're putting `use strict` in all of your programs, let's look at the class of run-time exceptions it can generate. One instance is from the use of *symbolic references*.

What's a symbolic reference? It's when a scalar contains a string that names another variable, and you attempt to use that scalar as though it were a *hard* reference. This works, if you're not using `strict` or have selectively disabled the component of `use strict` that prevents it.[3]

Now, in Perl 4, storing the name of a variable inside another variable was the only way to carry out certain very common tasks (and required that you also use `eval`). But since the advent of hard references in Perl 5, there is almost no situation in which you will need to use a symbolic reference. However, there may be many more occasions when you *think* that you need to. So let's examine some of those.

The program that follows is a hypothetical greengrocer's inventory counter that reads data consisting of a fruit or vegetable and the number of cases bought and sold of that item, separated by spaces on new lines.[4]

```
1   $fruit_cases_bought      = 0;
2   $fruit_cases_sold        = 0;
3   $vegetables_cases_bought = 0;
4   $vegetables_cases_sold   = 0;
5   %vegetable = map { ($_, 1) } qw(carrots broccoli
6                                       kale spinach leeks);
7   %fruit     = map { ($_, 1) } qw(apples kumquats
8                                       pears bananas kiwis);
9   while (<DATA>)
10      {
```

---

3. You do this with the statement `no strict 'refs'`.

4. Notice that we defied our own indenting style to put the `if` statement blocks on one line each, and left out the semicolon after their sole statements. This just goes to show that sometimes there's no need to be a slave to style if breaking the rules buys you an advantage like greater readability.

```
11     ($food, $cases_bought, $cases_sold) = split;
12     if (exists $vegetable{$food})  { $type = 'vegetable' }
13     elsif (exists $fruit{$food})   { $type = 'fruit'     }
14     else {   warn "I don't know the food type $food\n"   }
15
16     if (defined $type)
17         {
18         ${$type.'_cases_bought'} += $cases_bought;
19         ${$type.'_cases_sold'}   += $cases_sold;
20         }
21     }
22
23 print $vegetable_cases_bought - $vegetable_cases_sold,
24      " cases of vegetables on hand\n";
25
26 print $fruit_cases_bought - $fruit_cases_sold,
27      " cases of fruit on hand\n";
```

This kind of code is very common from a programmer who is happy to have identified the identical nature of the different sets of fruit and vegetable variables and abstracted their use to a degree that they can be summed with the same code. However, the symbolic references are not necessary: not only do they break use strict, but they do not work with lexical variables, which is why this program doesn't have any my keywords. Well, that doesn't sit right with Perl of Wisdom #8, so we should look for a way to write this program without dynamic variables.

We don't have to look far. Whenever you are tempted to create parallel variable sets, use instead a hash whose keys are the portion of your variable names that changes. Here's the new program:

```
1  my %cases_bought = (fruit => 0, vegetables => 0);
2  my %cases_sold   = (fruit => 0, vegetables => 0);
3  my %vegetable = map { ($_, 1) }
4                     qw(carrots broccoli kale spinach leeks);
5  my %fruit     = map { ($_, 1) }
6                     qw(apples kumquats pears bananas kiwis);
7
8  while (<>)
```

```
 9     {
10     my ($food, $bought, $sold) = split;
11     my $type;
12
13     if (exists $vegetable{$food}) { $type = 'vegetables' }
14     elsif (exists $fruit{$food})  { $type = 'fruit'      }
15     else { warn "I don't know the food type $food\n"    }
16
17     if (defined $type)
18        {
19        $cases_bought{$type} += $bought;
20        $cases_sold{$type}   += $sold;
21        }
22     }
23
24  foreach my $type (qw(fruit vegetables))
25     {
26     print $cases_bought{$type} - $cases_sold{$type},
27            " cases of $type on hand\n";
28     }
```

Now, if it looks obvious to you that this first example should be using a hash, be aware that it is easier to fall into this trap than you might think, especially when you have a large program with a bunch of hitherto disparate variables that you suddenly realize can be treated similarly.

Is this the best way to code this program? Hardly. We are repeating keys explicitly in two places where a typo would cause a problem. If we mistyped the strings in the $type assignment or the foreach—and it would be a natural mistake to type vegetable instead of vegetables—the program would still run, but it would not produce correct output.[5]

 Don't enter the same text in different places in a program and depend on having to keep them in sync.

---

5. It *would* generate a warning, courtesy of −w, in line 26 when we went to print a nonexistent hash entry, unless we were lucky enough to have mistyped vegetable in both places.

Or at the very least, we would like the code to refuse to run if we *did* make such a typo.

Perl 5.005 provides a new datatype—the *pseudo-hash*—which we can use here to accomplish that. In the following listing, it appears that little has changed structurally. But if you commit the typos we just discussed, instead of running, Perl instead spits out the error:

```
No such array field at greengrocer.pl line 16, <> chunk 1
```

even if we misspell vegetables in the same way on both line 11 and line 21.

```perl
 1  my $cases_bought = [{vegetables => 1, fruit => 2}, 0, 0];
 2  my $cases_sold   = [{vegetables => 1, fruit => 2}, 0, 0];
 3  my %vegetable = map { ($_, 1) } qw(carrots broccoli
 4                                     kale spinach leeks);
 5  my %fruit     = map { ($_, 1) } qw(apples kumquats
 6                                     pears bananas kiwis);
 7  while (<>)
 8     {
 9     my ($food, $bought, $sold) = split;
10     my $type;
11     if (exists $vegetable{$food})  { $type = 'vegetables' }
12     elsif (exists $fruit{$food})   { $type = 'fruit'      }
13     else { warn "I don't know the food type $food\n"      }
14     if (defined $type)
15        {
16        $cases_bought->{$type} += $bought;
17        $cases_sold->{$type}   += $sold;
18        }
19     }
20
21  foreach my $type (qw(fruit vegetables))
22     {
23     print $cases_bought->{$type} - $cases_sold->{$type},
24         " cases of $type on hand\n";
25     }
```

A pseudo-hash bears some explanation, since it's so new.[6] If the first element of an array is a reference to a hash, the other elements of that array can be accessed not just by their indices, but by using a reference to the array as though it were a hash reference whose keys were taken from that first element. The hash referenced by the first element must map the keys you wish to use to the indices of the values in the array. This is much easier to understand with an example:

```
$sound = [ { dog => 1, cat => 2, bird => 3},
           'bark', 'meow', 'tweet' ];
```

You must ensure that the numbers that are the values in the anonymous hash correspond to the positions of the corresponding values, but now you can say `$sound->{dog}` to yield `'bark'`. You could also get at it with `$sound->[1]`, but that's missing the point of a pseudo-hash. What you *can't* do is put a new key in the pseudo-hash in this fashion:

```
$sound->{frog} = 'ribbit';
```

because that will generate an error (putting a new key in the pseudo-hash is possible but harder than that). But if your application doesn't require inserting new keys at run time, this feature of the pseudo-hash will ensure that you are instantly alerted if you mistype a key.

Because pseudo-hashes have an uncertain future, we won't make a Perl of Wisdom out of them just yet. Evaluate the benefits of using them on a case-by-case basis. We have been making a more general point here that *is* worth a Perl of Wisdom:

Force as many errors as possible to occur at compile time rather than at run time.

---

6. As of perl version 5.005_03. It is not only new, it's experimental, so check the documentation for any version of Perl later than 5.6.0 that you have to see if it's still in there. It appears from the latest discussions that it is unlikely to survive to Perl 6; however, being able to create hashes whose keys are fixed is so useful that the capability to do this is likely to persist in some form.

This little program can be bulletproofed even further. It still requires the repetition of the keys vegetables and fruit in the pseudo-hashes and input recognition loop. If we could bind them together somehow, we'd have less of a chance of coming up with a compile-time error.

Enter our latest revision. Here we've done some more radical surgery. You'll notice that we've removed the need to refer to the hash keys while going around the input loop by creating the single hash %food_type to map from an inventory item to a vegetable or fruit.

```
 1  use fields;
 2  $_ = fields::phash(vegetables => 0, fruit => 0)
 3      for my ($cases_bought, my $cases_sold);
 4  my %food_type = (map ({ ($_, 'vegetables') }
 5                      qw(carrots broccoli kale spinach leeks)),
 6                      map { ($_, 'fruit') }
 7                      qw(apples kumquats pears bananas kiwis)
 8                     );
 9  while (<>)
10      {
11      my ($food, $bought, $sold) = split;
12      if (my $type = $food_type{$food})
13          {
14          $cases_bought->{$type} += $bought;
15          $cases_sold->{$type}   += $sold;
16          }
17        else
18          {
19          warn "I don't know the food type $food\n";
20          }
21      }
22
23  foreach my $type (keys %$cases_bought)
24      {
25      print $cases_bought->{$type} - $cases_sold->{$type},
26          " cases of $type on hand\n";
27      }
```

We used a function new to Perl 5.6.0, fields::phash, which takes the sting out of creating pseudo-hashes, and at the same time avoids the repetition we had on the first two lines of our previous version. If pseudo-hashes are retained in later versions of Perl but their implementation alters, `fields::phash` will be changed to hide that implementation change from you. When we want to iterate over the different food types to print our report, we just use the keys of a pseudo-hash (which means we no longer get to pick the order, unless we sort the keys).

9.2 Check That Return Code!

The Perl built-in functions that might fail return a special value to alert you that they have done so. Usually, this value is false. (Functions that call out to the operating system to do their work will put the type of error in the $! variable.) This allows a number of common colloquialisms for checking and handling it, the most famous of which is the open-or-die idiom:

```
open DICT, '/usr/dict/words'
    or die "I'm at a loss for words: $!";
```

This being Perl, there are many other ways of expressing the same thing. Pick one that works for you:

```
if (mkdir $tmpdir, 0755)
   {
   copy $dbfile, "$tmpdir/$dbfile.$$"
   }
else
   {
   die "Couldn't create $tmpdir because $!";
   }

die "Can't chdir to $subdir: $!" unless chdir $subdir;

print chmod (0644, @files) ? "Success!" : "Failure: $!";
```

You're not required to stick to only one idiom, mind you. It's common for people to choose different ones according to the way they think about the operation they're expressing.

You have to be fanatical about checking return codes if you want to write quality programs. For instance, in the first example in the preceding list, the copy function from File::Copy also returns true or false and sets $! on failure. It would be a strange sort of program that wouldn't have a reason to ensure that this had happened.

Some functions return something besides true/false but still set $!, for example, chmod, chown, and unlink each take a list of files to operate upon, return the number of files actually modified, and if there were any errors, set $! to the last one. (Unfortunately it's not possible to tell which file(s) had problems without checking manually afterwards.)

29 Know your operating system.

 A student in one of my classes encountered the following. The assignment was to create a temporary directory and a bunch of files in it, perform some operations on them, and then to remove the files and the directory. Part of his code looked something like this:

```
foreach my $file (@files)
   {
   open OUT, ">$file" or die "Can't open $file: $!\n";
   # write something to the file
   }

# Open the files in the directory and do something
# with the contents

die "Unlink didn't get everything: $!\n" unless
                          unlink @files == @files;
chdir '..' or die "Couldn't go up a level: $!\n";
rmdir $tmpdir or die "Couldn't rmdir $tmpdir: $!\n";
```

> Every return code dutifully checked, but the `rmdir` failed, and `$!` said, "Directory not empty." Yet when he looked in the directory, there were no files there. What was going wrong?
>
> The problem was that he had omitted the `close` statement from the loop that created the files. Whenever Perl encounters an `open` statement using an existing filehandle, it closes that filehandle for you, so all but the last file had already been closed. On Unix, if any process has a file open, it is not removed by `unlink` until the file is closed, so the last file in `@files` had not been removed at the time the `rmdir` was executed. But then the program exited, which meant that all its open filehandles were closed; at that point the file was removed, destroying the evidence.

Other operating systems may handle this case differently. Because Perl uses the underlying operating system, you must be familiar with the quirks and gotchas that apply there too.

In case you think it unlikely you'd write a program that created files and then removed them in the same invocation, think about temporary storage or checkpoint/restart capability.

9.3 Taking Exception to Yourself

Having discussed how we handle exceptions generated by Perl, it's time to talk about how we make exceptions of our own. You're already used to the most basic exception-generating method, which is to call `die`. The arguments are printed, and your program exits with a nonzero return code. (Just *which* nonzero return code is documented in gory detail under `perldoc -f die`.)

You may see some additional text output by die, such as the line number of code it died on. If instead it says (eval 13), it's telling you that it was executing the thirteenth call to eval and prints the line number relative to the evaled code, not the program containing the eval. If it says <FOO> chunk 42, it means that you had the filehandle FOO open and had made 42 calls to the readline function (or <>) on it. If you didn't change the $/ variable so that readline read more than one line at a time, newer Perls will say <FOO> line 42 instead.

Maybe you're tired of tacking ' or die...' onto every system call and just want it to happen automatically. Well, as of version 5.005_03, you can use Lionel Cons and Ilya Zakharevich's Fatal.pm and just specify for which routines you want this magical behavior to occur. Just list them in the use statement:

```
use Fatal qw(open mkdir chdir);
```

The routines have to be *overridable*, which is not something easily determined by mortals (translation: you have to look at the source). Bottom line: to see if it works, try it out on any core function you want to use it on first.

Note that while you can do this for any function (including your own), it's not useful for the ones like chmod, which return the number of files modified (unless you're only ever going to modify one file at a time). Although you can't use it on the exec or system calls (for esoteric reasons), if you could, it wouldn't be any good on system because that call returns 0 in the event of success.

9.4 Playing Catch-Up

Let's say that you want to go in the other direction and instead of turning errors into exceptions, you want to know when your program is about to die. The brute-force approach is to define a pseudo signal handler for __DIE__:

```
$SIG{__DIE__} = sub { print "Igor lives!\n" };
```

but this is rather ineffectual for several reasons. First, we don't know *why* the program is dying (without parsing the argument, which is an arbitrary string). Second, we don't know *where* the program is dying without parsing the line number out of the argument (but when you think about it, that information is absolutely useless *inside* your program). And third, the Faustian bargain that this handler has made lasts only as long as it does; as soon as the handler exits, your program dies anyway.[7]

Fortunately, there is an approach that solves two of these problems at the same time, which is to use the block form of the `eval` operator. Put the code you want to check on in the block, and if anything inside it causes it to `die`, Perl will transfer control to the end of the block and put the message from `die` in the special variable `$@`. For example,

```
my %dotfiles;
while (my ($username, $home) = (getpwent)[0,7])
   {
   eval
      {
      opendir HOME, $home or die "$home: $!";
      foreach (grep -f && /^\./, readdir HOME)
         {
         open DOT, "$home/$_" or die "$_: $!";
         $dotfiles{$username}{$_} = () = <DOT>;
         close DOT;
         }
      closedir HOME;
      };   # Note the semicolon that is required here
   if ($@)
      {
      print "Problem with $username, reason: $@";
      }
   }
```

_____

7. Unlike real signal handlers, which return to whatever code was executing when the signal arrived.

Because we get to choose how much or how little code goes inside the `eval` block, we can determine the granularity with which we trap exceptions. This code—which is building a hash-of-hashes containing line counts of dot files in users' home directories—uses `eval` to catch two possible exceptions (the failure to open a directory or a file, respectively) and then keeps going. To bail out as soon as we hit any problem, we would wrap the `eval` around the `while` loop.

A program will not exit if it dies for some reason while under the care of an `eval` block. However, we still have to parse `$@` after the block to find out why an exception occurred, if there were multiple possible causes.

What's useful about this method of exception handling is that inside the `eval` block, we could be calling subroutines to any depth, be deep inside a horrible mixture of our code and someone else's libraries, and have no idea what might be going on inside them; however, if any statement in them issues a `die`, it will get caught by that `eval` block.

 Bullet-proof your program by trapping exceptions and handling them gracefully.

Let's stop beating around the bush. What we really want is the ability to type exceptions and preferably also to subclass them, then catch them according to class while passing along instance-specific data.[8] Just like in Java. While we're at it, it should use the same `try ... throw ... catch` syntax.

It seems that the Perl mascot could just as well be a chameleon as a camel, since it can take on so many colors. An implementation of the `try ... throw ... catch` capability is in the module `Error.pm` by Graham Barr, on CPAN (`http://search.cpan.org/search?dist=Error`). It allows you to write things like

---

8. Not everyone thinks this way, just to be fair. If you'd rather stick with `die... eval`, you'll be in plenty of company.

```
try
    {
    # Some relational database-munging code. Somewhere
    # inside this something might raise an exception with
    # a line like:
    throw Exception::SQL (-text => 'Bad SELECT statement');
    }
catch Exception::SQL with
    {
    # Code to handle SQL exceptions
    }
catch Exception::IO with
    {
    # Code to handle I/O exceptions
    }
otherwise
    {
    # Code to handle other kinds of exceptions
    };
```

Exception::SQL and Exception::IO are classes of exception that
we created earlier by the simple expediency of inheriting from Error itself:

```
@Exception::SQL::ISA = 'Error';
@Exception::IO::ISA  = 'Error';
```

An alternative to Error.pm is Brad Appleton's AtExit CPAN module
(http://search.cpan.org/search?dist=AtExit), which allows
you to specify a handler routine to be executed whenever the current scope is
left for any reason, similar to the C++ auto_ptr template class. For instance:

```
use AtExit;
...
    {
    # Code to acquire a database connection
    atexit(\&cleanup);
    # More database code which might fail
    }
```

This ensures that no matter how that code block is exited, the `cleanup` subroutine to break the connection gracefully will be run.

9.5 Confession Is Good for the Soul

Sometimes your program dies not in your code but in some module you call—suicide by association if you will. A module that wants to `die` is supposed to call `Carp::croak` instead, because `croak` reports the location of death as the place the module function was called, not the line of code in the module function containing the `croak` call.

Some modules don't do this. Either they call `die`, or they call another module that `croak`s; either way, you're left with an error message that doesn't tell you which line of your program caused its untimely demise.

If this happens, here's a quick way to force it to 'fess up. Near the beginning of your program, insert the following:

```
use Carp qw(cluck verbose);
$SIG{__DIE__}  = sub { confess @_ };
$SIG{__WARN__} = sub { cluck @_ };
```

Now whenever your program calls `die`/`croak` or carp/`warn` it ends up calling `confess` or `cluck`[9] instead, which have exactly the same effect except they print a stack trace of how they were called that goes all the way back to your main program.

---

9. Perl is nothing if not whimsical. Presumably in this case it helps to dispel the air of morbidity surrounding the whole topic of program death.

Chapter 10

Semantical Errors

"Pay attention even to trifles."

A Book of Five Rings, *by Miyamoto Musashi*

Semantical errors are a way of saying that when all else succeeds, you can still be wrong. The program compiles; it runs without any kind of run-time exception; it just doesn't do what you intended. This is why you need system testing (see Chapter 6).

(If you're relatively new to Perl, this chapter might raise the hairs on the back of your neck a little. Feel free to return to it after you've gotten more comfortable with the language.) Here's a tour of some examples of this obnoxious species of bug.

10.1 A Bit Illogical

Perl has several ways of saying *and* and *or*:

TABLE 10-1. *And*, *Or*, and *Xor* Operators in Perl

Operation	AND	OR	XOR
bitwise (non-short-circuiting)	&	|	^
logical (high precedence)	&&	||	
logical (low precedence)	and	or	xor

(There is no high-precedence logical XOR operator.) The consequences of picking an operator from the wrong row are usually annoying mistakes like

```
open (FH, $file) | die "Error opening $file: $!\n";
```

which dies whether or not the open succeeds, because the | operator is strictly a bitwise arithmetic or string operator, which evaluates both of its operands so that it can return the result of ORing their bits together. In this case, you want ||, which is a logical operator that evaluates its left-hand side and returns it if true; otherwise it evaluates and returns its right-hand side.

An even better choice would be the `or` operator introduced in Perl 5, which has such low precedence that you can leave out the parentheses on `open`:

```
open FH, $file or die "Error opening $file: $!\n";
```

10.2 Reading Directories

This has bitten us more times than we care to admit:

31 **`readdir()` returns the list of filenames in the directory, but they are not qualified by the directory itself.**

Consider the following program:

```
use strict;
use File::stat;

my $dir = shift || '.';
opendir DIR, $dir or die "Error opening directory $dir: $!\n";
while (defined (my $file = readdir DIR))
    {
    print "File $file was last modified on "
          . localtime(stat($file)->mtime), "\n";
    }
closedir DIR;
```

It takes a directory as its argument, defaulting to the current directory. This program prints out the names and modification times of all the files in the current directory.

If run with no arguments, the program runs fine. If we then run it with an argument (this example is on Unix), it appears to start working and then fails:

```
File . was last modified on Sun Mar 28 14:36:27 1999
File .. was last modified on Tue Aug  3 15:29:12 1999
```

```
Can't call method "mtime" without a package or object reference
at mod_times.pl line 9.
```

What happened here?

First, we see the error refers to line 9 and that perl attempted to invoke the `mtime` method on something that wasn't even an object. What was the object? It was the result of the call to `stat($file)` (we're using the `stat` routine from the `File::stat` module here, instead of the core perl `stat` routine that returns a list; it saves us from having to look up the index of the `mtime` element).

The specification of that function says that if `$file` doesn't exist, `stat` returns `undef`, which certainly isn't an object. Therefore `$file` doesn't exist. And the reason it doesn't exist is because `$file` doesn't contain an absolute path and therefore is interpreted relative to the current directory. The current directory won't contain files with the same names as the ones we read with `readdir` except by coincidence and except (on Unix) for the two files that every directory contains (`.` and `..`). This is why we get some initial output that makes it look as though the script is working. It isn't; it's reporting the times for different `.` and `..` from the ones we wanted.

The fix is easy: just qualify `$file` with `$dir`:

```
use strict;
use File::stat;

my $dir = shift || '.';
opendir DIR, $dir or die "Error opening directory $dir: $!\n";
while (defined (my $file = readdir DIR)) {
  print "File $file was last modified on "
        . localtime(stat("$dir/$file")->mtime), "\n";
}
closedir DIR;
```

This works even if $dir is relative or contains ../.[1]

10.3 But What Did It Mean?

The following program is designed to reprint its input lines prefixed with an increasing date that skips weekends:

```perl
#!/usr/bin/perl -w
use strict;
use Time::Local;
my $t = timelocal(0,0,0,31,11,99);    # Dec 31 1999
while (<>)
   {
   my ($m, $d, $y) = (localtime $t)[4,3,5];
   $y %= 100;
   $m++;
   print "$m/$d/$y $_";
   dp { $t += 86400 } while (localtime $t)[6] == 0
                         || (localtime $t)[6] == 6;
   }
```

However, the output shows a date that doesn't change:

```
12/31/99 This is the first line
12/31/99 This is the second line
12/31/99 This is the third line
```

Running under the debugger won't reveal anything other than the fact that $t isn't being increased in the do block.

Wait a minute. It doesn't say do, does it? It's a typo: dp. Yes, we could fix the program right now. But curiosity demands that we wonder why Perl has no objections! What could it be thinking we mean?

---

1. Using / as a directory separator works on Unix and Windows (Perl turns it into a \ on the latter). A truly operating system-independent way of forming the path would use File::Spec and replace "$dir/$file" with File::Spec->catfile($dir, $file);

Enter the B::Deparse module. The B stands for "back-end," which is to say, this module accepts input from the Perl compiler after it has created a binary opcode tree from a program. The whole purpose in life of B::Deparse is to turn that opcode tree back into Perl. For instance, you can use it to turn a subroutine reference into program text in the middle of a program.

Deparse isn't quite perfect—you may see some odd output, at times even incorrect output—but it's getting there.[2] Let's see what we get when we run it on just a part of the line of code that's bugging us. Notice that we don't invoke it with a use statement but rather with a funny variant of the -M option designed for back-end modules:

```
% perl -MO=Deparse -e 'dp { $t += 86400 } while \
                       (localtime $t)[6] == 0'
do { $t += 86400 }->dp while (localtime $t)[6] == 0;
-e syntax OK
```

Aha! Perl is interpreting our typo as a use of the indirect object method syntax—it thinks we want to call the dp method of whatever the block $t += 86400 evaluates to. So this is no longer a do *BLOCK* while *EXPRESSION* construct (which guarantees the block will be executed at least once). Instead it is a *STATEMENT* while *EXPRESSION* construct (where the statement is do { $t += 86400 }->dp), which means that the statement will be executed only if the expression is true, which in this case, it isn't to begin with.

The Deparse module can often explain how perl is parsing your code.

Note: Deparse only came into the core with version 5.005, and it's documentation has some additional options worth checking out, like the ability to totally parenthesize expressions so you can see how precedence is determined. (And if you see '???' in the output, that stands for a constant in the input that

---

2. Larry Wall said that Perl 6 should be translatable into Perl 5 via a kind of Deparse module, so we can expect considerable progress.

was optimized by perl to the point where its value was not available to `Deparse`.)

Here's another example in which `Deparse` helps. Let's say you're scanning text to pull out URLs and want to clean them up a little by removing redundant default port numbers:

```perl
my %port = (http => 80,  https  => 443, ftp => 79,
            nntp => 119, gopher => 70);
while (<DATA>)
    {
    if (my ($url) = m#((\w+)://\S+[\w])#)
        {
        $url = ~ s#:$port{$2}/#/# if $port{$2};
        print "URL found: $url\n";
        }
    }
```

(Yes, there are better ways of isolating URLs from text; this code doesn't even find more than one per line. But that's not the point we're about to make.)

Flushed with the cleverness of our code, we feed it the input:

```
The President (http://www.whitehouse.gov:80/president/) \
    said today that he
liked ferrets (http://www.ferretcentral.org/), and was
considering placing a picture of one (ftp://ftp.optics.\
    rochester.edu:79/pub/pgreene/icons/central-logo-t.gif)
on the next version of the national flag; but he
thought they were too often confused with gophers
(gopher://gopher.tc.umn.edu:70/11/).
```

expecting to see the output:[3]

---

3. We indented continuation lines in the input and output to make them easier to read.

```
URL found: http://www.whitehouse.gov/president/
URL found: http://www.ferretcentral.org
URL found: ftp://ftp.optics.rochester.edu/pub/pgreene/\
  icons/central-logo-t.gif
URL found: gopher://gopher.tc.umn.edu/11
```

But instead, we see:

```
URL found: 4294967294
URL found: 4294967295
URL found: 4294967294
URL found: 4294967294
```

If you run this program through `Deparse`, you'll see the line

```
$url = ~s[:$port{$2}/][/] if $port{$2};
```

which gives us just enough of a clue if we haven't found the typo already. The space we accidentally put inside the regex binding operator has changed its meaning to "`$url` is assigned the one's complement of the result of this substitution on `$_` (which in a scalar context is the number of substitutions made)."

10.3.1 Flashback...

Remember in Chapter 8 we wondered why Perl placed the error with the transposed `for` clauses on the wrong line? Now we know how to find out!

```
$ perl -MO=Deparse temp.pl
Useless use of numeric lt (<) in void context at temp.pl line
13.
my $fmt = '%10s ' x 5;
printf "$fmt\n", qw(Kelvin Celsius Rankine
                    Fahrenheit Reaumur);
$fmt = '%10.2f ' x 5;
my $kelvin = 0;
while ($kelvin += 10)
   {
```

```
    my $celsius = $kelvin - 273.15;
    my $rankine = $kelvin * 9 / 5;
    my $fahrenheit = $rankine - 459.67;
    my $reaumur = $celsius * 4 / 5;
    printf "$fmt\n", $kelvin, $celsius, $rankine,
                     $fahrenheit, $reaumur;
    }
continue
    {
    $kelvin < 500
}
```

Well, look at that. The dirty truth about `for` loops emerges: they're nothing but `while` loops in fancy clothes. The test clause got relocated to a `continue` block, where, of course, it makes no sense, being an expression in void context.

10.4 `printf` *Formats Don't Impose Context*

If you're a die-hard C programmer (and is there any other kind?), you might think that to print the number of entries in an array, since the `%d` `printf` format specifier means "number," well gosh, a number is a scalar, and so that's the context it'll put its argument into:

```
printf "Number of entries in \@foo = %d", @foo;
```

but by now you know us too well to fall for that... yes, `@foo` is in list context here, because that's what `printf` is prototyped to take. So you'll either get the first entry of `@foo` printed, or a complaint if that's not a number.

10.5 *Conditional* my

You have a subroutine that should set a private variable based on some condition. Not unreasonably, you might code something following this general form:

```
sub ordinal
   {
   my $what = shift;
   my $res = 'first'  if $what == 1;
   $res    = 'second' if $what == 2;
   return $res;
   }
```

But you'd be wrong. If we run this through `perl -l` with `for (1..3) {`
`print ordinal($_) }`, we get the result:

```
first
second
second
```

Eh? Shouldn't that last line be a warning about an undefined value? Regrettably, you've fallen afoul of an internal optimization in Perl[4] that keeps the storage assigned to lexical variables around after they're gone, on the premise that they may be needed again shortly. The `my` statement has both a compile-time effect (declaring the variable) and a run-time effect (setting it to `undef`, unless the statement is qualified by a failed condition).

33 **Never qualify a `my` statement with a condition.**

Note that this is not talking about putting `my` statements *inside* conditions:

```
if ((my $tag = $element->tag) ne 'p')
   {
   # Code using $tag
   }

while (my ($key, $value) = each %hash) { ... }
```

which is a very good idiom in that it concisely limits the scope of the new variable to precisely the block in which you need it.

----

4. That may change in a future version.

10.6 Bringing Some Closure

Understanding how lexical variables work is worth the effort. Suppose you have advanced to the stage of understanding closures—give yourself a pat on the back—and you decide to code a few subroutines that use a private variable that way:

```
{
my $protocol = "ftp";   # default

sub get_proto
   {
   return $protocol;
   }
sub set_proto
   {
   $protocol = shift;
   }
}   # End of block containing closures

print get_proto();
```

(We've removed anything not necessary to understanding this point.) If you run this, you'll see that it indeed knows what the default protocol is, and you've successfully isolated that shared variable to the two subroutines that use it.

Let's say that later you decide that the subroutines are better off declared at the end of the file so that you can start reading with your main program—Perl can handle forward references, right? So you change it to

```
print get_proto();
   {
   my $protocol = "ftp";   # default

   sub get_proto
      {
      return $protocol;
      }
```

```
sub set_proto
   {
   $protocol = shift;
   }
}   # End of block containing closures
```

But now when you run the program, `get_proto` will complain about an uninitialized variable. The reason is closely related to our previous error: when we call `get_proto` in the first line, `$protocol` hasn't been initialized because we haven't gotten to the line where that happens yet. The reason there's no complaint from `strict` about it being an undeclared variable in the closures is that it *has* been declared; however, that happened at *compile* time, and the assignment of the default value won't happen until *run* time.

You can avoid this problem naturally by following Perl of Wisdom #18. If you don't yet understand closures but you're intrigued, read "What's a closure?" in the core Perl documentation section `perlfaq7`.

Chapter 11

Resource Failure

"He's dead, Jim."

Dr. Leonard McCoy in Star Trek: The Devil in the Dark

Computer scientists talk knowledgeably about "Turing-complete" programming languages, by which they mean a language that can be shown to be equivalent to a Turing machine and therefore provably able to solve any computation that can be expressed as an algorithm. A Turing machine is a hypothetical device invented by Alan Turing, and consists of a long tape passing under a read/write head that is capable of reading and printing characters on the tape according to a table of rules specifying what to do.

Unfortunately, no implementation of any programming language does or ever could live up to the strict definition of "Turing-complete," since Turing specified that his machine was equipped with an infinitely long tape. He also specified that the machine was allowed an arbitrary amount of time to solve a problem, which is a luxury that few people outside of academia can afford.

This chapter is about what to do when your finite resources are too finite. We'll discuss how to react when you run out of time, memory, or disk space.

11.1 Optimize for People First, Resources Later

Note that we didn't say, "... how to *avoid* running out of ...." There's a good reason for this: If you worry about it from the beginning, you're optimizing for the wrong thing. While you'll see a lot of carping from seasoned professionals on Usenet arguing that such-and-such code isn't as efficient as their latest mutation of it, understand that they're coming from a place where the mind-bending code they've just written is as clear to them as anything else. More often than not, they're coming up with these performance enhancements to make the problem more interesting for themselves.

They would not disagree with the advice we're about to give, however:

 Optimize your code for readability and maintainability first; make performance optimizations only after profiling of a working version demands it.

By far the most dominant resource cost in software today is not CPU speed, RAM, or disk space; it's people. The time spent by people developing, documenting, maintaining, inheriting, reading, porting, modifying, enhancing, understanding, or debugging an application is the most precious and scarce resource in information technology. Therefore our advice up to this point has focused on how to develop applications to make the best use of that time.

Also, don't underestimate the ability of Moore's Law to help you. In other words, if you're developing an application that will not be operational for another year and a half, by that time processors will be twice as fast, RAM will be half the price, and disk drives will be twice as big. If you're able to trade developer time for procurement dollars (and it's strange how many companies devalue their employees' time in comparison to their hardware even though their bank account doesn't know the difference) and the problem can be solved more cheaply by better hardware, get it.

There will be plenty of other opportunities to practice writing efficient programs because sometimes you really won't have enough resources to run them, and then you will have to make them do better. Whatever you are developing, though, don't assume you know in advance what resource you may run out of. The aforementioned seasoned professionals know that the ability of even the best of them to predict such things is notoriously unreliable.[1]

We will show how you can optimize your programs for speed, memory, or disk space. However, these are not independent variables; frequently there are trade-offs (e.g., gaining memory at the expense of disk space). Equally common are parallel gains: For instance, as you improve your code style, memory usage may go down and execution speed may go up due to fewer memory accesses.

---

1. This is not to say that there aren't occasions when resource limitations are fairly obvious. If you're archiving the entire World Wide Web, you should probably be concerned about disk space before you start. (If you *are* archiving the entire World Wide Web using Perl, please drop us a line; we have a few questions to ask you.)

11.2 Benchmark It!

Because it's generally so hard to tell by looking at the code where the bottle-necks are (especially since they may move depending on your hardware configuration), you have to be able to measure them objectively. You may have no recourse but to use the native tools of your operating system to measure virtual memory usage in particular. (See Perl of Wisdom #29.) In this respect we confess we are far more experienced on the various Unix platforms than on the Macintosh or Windows.[2]

11.2.1 Measuring Memory Usage

The `top` program available on most Unix variants is very good for determining how much processor time and virtual memory are being used by current processes. To gather the same information from inside a script, or if your `top` is restricted for `root`'s use only, use the `ps` program to get information about the process numbered `pid`. On SYSVish systems, use `ps -lp pid`; on BSDish systems, use `ps u pid`. (You can usually use a repeated `-w` flag on SYSV or a `w` flag on BSD to see more of the command column if it is truncated.)

In each case, there are two columns labeled `SZ` (or `VSZ`) and `RSS`. Roughly speaking, these are, respectively, the total virtual memory in use by the process and the amount of physical memory in use, both in kilobytes. Note that the amount of memory allocated by a Unix process never decreases before it terminates; whenever it frees memory it makes it available only for the same process to reuse again later. (It is not returned to the free pool for other processes to use.)

---

2. We tried measuring process size on Windows 98 using a freeware tool called `prcview` and were baffled by the results. It appeared that every process out of a couple of dozen was using at least 20 MB.

A very large and lengthy program of mine that reports its girth hourly has just displayed

```
USER    PID %CPU %MEM   SZ   RSS  TT S START    TIME   COMMAND
peter 28679 51.9 48.5 35248 30072 ?  S 08:42:02 279:33 [trun-
cated]
```

which shows that its total memory usage is 35 MB, 30 of which are in physical memory. (The output was doctored slightly since the columns output by `ps` had actually run together.) Because it has had problems with running out of memory, this provides periodic statistics that tell me what it really uses.

If you want to monitor the progress of your own Perl script, use $$ in place of `pid`:

```
printf "Current virtual memory: %sk\n", unpack '@24A5',
       (`ps u $$`)[1];
```

(The actual `unpack` template you have to use may be different for your `ps`. By using a subscript on the backticks in list context, we can ignore the header line output by `ps`.) You can use `ps` like this to see the actual amount of memory used by your program as it executes. (And remember that on Unix, process sizes never decrease, no matter how much memory you free in your program. Your process will never get smaller than its largest memory allocation.)

Under MacOS, access "About This Computer" from the Apple menu. A graphic displays the allocated memory per process and the fraction used (see Figure 11-1).

FIGURE 11-1. Memory usage under MacOS

11.2.2 Measuring CPU usage

The same `ps` or `top` commands will also tell you how much cpu and elapsed time a process has used, of course. You can also use the Unix `time` command to tell you the same thing:

```
$ time myprog
0.050u 0.180s 0:03.68 6.2%      0+0k 0+0io 98pf+0w
```

This tells you that `myprog` took 3.68 seconds of realtime to run, but spent only 0.05 + 0.18 = 0.23 seconds using the CPU (it must have been doing a lot of I/O).

But what if you want to find the fastest strategy among several choices? You could run each one separately and time them, of course. Fortunately, Perl can do it for you with the `Benchmark` module, by Jarkko Hietaniemi and Tim Bunce. Let's say that you're initializing a large hash inside a loop that gets executed many times and you want to know whether it's faster to use a hash slice or a foreach loop:

```
use Benchmark;
timethese (400,
          { undef   => '@h{1..10000} = ()',
            set     => '@h{1..10000} = (1)x10000',
            loop    => '$h{$_} = undef for 1..10000',
            loopset => '$h{$_} = 1 for 1..10000',
          });
```

The results from this are:[3]

```
Benchmark: timing 400 iterations of loop, loopset, set, undef..
.
    loop: 21 wallclock secs (21.07 usr +  0.01 sys =
                             21.08 CPU)
 loopset: 21 wallclock secs (21.03 usr +  0.00 sys =
                             21.03 CPU)
     set: 17 wallclock secs (16.44 usr +  0.01 sys =
                             16.45 CPU)
   undef:  8 wallclock secs ( 7.58 usr +  0.00 sys =
                              7.58 CPU)
```

Note that the tests are run in alphabetical order by name, not necessarily in the order they were specified; that's because they're hash keys, and hashes have no innate ordering.

If the code you're testing does little or no I/O, the figures you should compare are the CPU times; the wall clock figures can be skewed if the machine is busy servicing other processes. If you're testing different code snippets that do lots of I/O, and do that I/O differently, then you have more of a problem. You

---

3. We're leaving out some redundant parts of the output that would make it harder to read here.

have no choice except to compare wall clock figures, but you must make sure that the system isn't interrupted by some other large process while you are benchmarking. So keep an eye on it with `top` or the equivalent to see what else is running during your benchmark.

We can see that there's no difference in setting an element to `undef` or `1`, but there *is* a significant improvement in setting all the elements at once to `1` with a hash slice and an even bigger improvement in using a hash slice to set them all to `undef` (presumably because we aren't taking the time to form a large list on the right-hand side). This tidbit can come in handy when we're using a hash just to test for existence; we can set the keys using a hash slice without having to set the values and later test for existence with `exists`.

Well, wait a minute. Might there be a performance hit from using the `exists` function rather than testing the truth of the hash value? Why guess when we can benchmark it?

```
use Benchmark;
my %h;
@h{map int rand 1000, 1..100} = (1) x 100;
timethese (1000000,
          { exists => '$x++ if exists $h{int rand 1000}',
            true   => '$x++ if $h{int rand 1000}',
          });
```

We first fill the hash with up to 100 integer keys randomly chosen from the range 0 to 999, and then we compare the operation of testing an element for existence with testing one for truth. (The `$x++` is just to give Perl something to do so we don't have to worry about whether a smart optimizer might decide to elide our code altogether.) The results are

```
Benchmark: timing 1000000 iterations of exists, true...
    exists:  7 wallclock secs ( 6.52 usr +  0.02 sys =
                               6.54 CPU)
      true:  7 wallclock secs ( 6.28 usr +  0.00 sys =
                               6.28 CPU)
```

There is no (significant) difference.

 35 ## Use the `Benchmark` module to compare the relative speeds of different code strategies.

What else can we learn from this Perl of Wisdom? Well, you may be wondering why there was no complaint in the first `Benchmark` example about the hash %h not being declared. We can infer from section 3.6.1 (pointing out that `use strict` is lexically scoped) that `Benchmark` evaluates each chunk of code in a lexical scope that is separate from the one enclosing it. So if the code you're testing is long enough to be worth `strict` checking, put `use strict` at the beginning of each chunk. This scoping effect also means that any lexical variables you declare in the main program won't be visible inside the benchmark code chunks.

We should point out that there is rarely any point to benchmarking code that isn't going to be run many, many times by your program. So if it's just code that's going to be run once, don't bother benchmarking it unless it either (a) takes a really, really long time or (b) needs to run very, very quickly (e.g., has to respond to a user in real time).

Benchmarking needs careful thought and can be an art. Benchmark the wrong thing, and the conclusion you draw can easily be the opposite of the right one. Suppose you're benchmarking code that uses a constant function inside a loop. If you put the definition in the code chunk, it'll get executed once for each iteration, whereas in your program it will get executed only once. The difference between the two approaches is seen in this benchmark, which shows how the result is changed by putting the constant definition in the loop:

```
use constant OUTSTR => 'The cat sat on the mat';
timethese(10000000,
    {
    inconst   => q(use constant INSTR   =>
                        'The cat sat on the mat';
                 INSTR   =~ /cat/),
    outconst => q(OUTSTR =~ /cat/),
```

```
    });

  inconst: 31 wallclock secs (31.27 usr +  0.00 sys =
                               31.27 CPU)
 outconst: 29 wallclock secs (28.78 usr +  0.00 sys =
                               28.78 CPU)
```

Notice how we used the q() operator instead of '...' to make a visual block out of the code chunks.

So make the code you benchmark as close as possible to what you will actually use in production. Make sure the machine is not heavily loaded, because a really busy machine could spend so much time keeping its house in order that it would skew the CPU figure. Therefore, make benchmarks short enough that you can keep an eye on the system with top or the equivalent while they're running, and so you can run them again to ensure that the results are consistent.

11.2.3 Ask de Prof

Our discussion of Benchmark presumes that you know where the critical regions of your code are. After all, if you have a subroutine that consumes only 1% of the time used by your program, no amount of optimization therein will improve your overall performance by more than 1%.

One way of finding out where your program spends the most time is with the Devel::DProf module. To see it in action, we'll construct a very simple program to count different types of file on our system:

```
use strict;
my ($symlinks, $dirs, $regulars,
    $sockets, $blocks, $chars, $others) = (0) x 7;
doit ('/');
print <<"EOF";
Symlinks: $symlinks, Dirs: $dirs, Regulars: $regulars
Sockets: $sockets, Blocks: $blocks, Chars: $chars, Others:
$others
EOF
```

```
sub doit
   {
   my $dir = shift;
   opendir DIR, $dir or return;
   my @files = grep !/^\.\.?$/, readdir DIR;
   closedir DIR;
   $dir = '' if $dir eq '/';
   process("$dir/$_") for @files;
   doit($_) for grep ! -l, grep -d, map "$dir/$_", @files;
   }

sub process
   {
   local $_ = shift;
   -l && return sym($_);
   -d && return dir($_);
   -f && return regular($_);
   -S && return sock($_);
   -b && return block($_);
   -c && return char($_);
   return       other($_);
   }

sub sym     { $symlinks++ }
sub dir     { $dirs++     }
sub regular { $regulars++ }
sub sock    { $sockets++  }
sub block   { $blocks++   }
sub char    { $chars++    }
sub other   { $others++   }
```

This code is purposely broken out into subroutines rather than the more obvious data-driven solution of using a hash keyed by stat flags to illustrate how Devel::DProf works. (Note that we again eschewed our usual brace style in the file type counting subroutines in favor of something more compact and more readable in this case.)

You may be wondering why there is no mention of Devel::DProf in the source code; the answer is that this is a special module that is invoked by the −d option as an alternate debugger module. (So instead of the default module,

which presents a command-line interface for stepping through your program,
`Devel::DProf` basically intercepts subroutine calls[4] and starts a stopwatch.
) This is how we run it:

```
$ perl -d:DProf dirwalk
Symlinks: 1804, Dirs: 4519, Regulars: 67319
Sockets: 7, Blocks: 3467, Chars: 1856, Others: 50
```

This creates a file `tmon.out` (you can change the name with the environment variable `PERL_DPROF_OUT_FILE_NAME`) in the current directory and
puts raw tracing information in it. The tool that can cook that information into
something palatable for you is `dprofpp`:

```
$ dprofpp
Total Elapsed Time = 25.03237 Seconds
  User+System Time = 24.83237 Seconds
Exclusive Times
%Time ExclSec CumulS #Calls sec/call Csec/c  Name
 81.1   20.14 20.755  79022   0.0003 0.0003  main::process
 28.8   7.157 146.90   4520   0.0016 0.0325  main::doit
 9.05   2.248  1.678  67319   0.0000 0.0000  main::regular
 0.56   0.140  0.102   4519   0.0000 0.0000  main::dir
 0.36   0.090  0.061   3467   0.0000 0.0000  main::block
 0.28   0.070  0.055   1804   0.0000 0.0000  main::sym
 0.16   0.040  0.024   1856   0.0000 0.0000  main::char
 0.04   0.010  0.010      1   0.0100 0.0100  main::BEGIN
 0.00   0.000 -0.000      1   0.0000      -  strict::import
 0.00   0.000 -0.000     50   0.0000      -  main::other
 0.00   0.000 -0.000      7   0.0000      -  main::sock
 0.00   0.000 -0.000      1   0.0000      -  strict::bits
```

We could have executed the script with `dprofpp` and then interpreted the
results by entering the single command `dprofpp -p dirwalk`; unfortunately, it would still have generated the `tmon.out` file. We would like to see

---

4. Unfortunately, it is not possible to profile on a finer granularity than subroutines.

an option for `Devel::DProf` to pipe its output into `dprofpp` to eliminate the temporary file.

Warning: The `tmon.out` file can get extraordinarily large very quickly (the one for the previous test was 1.3MB). Before you run a large test, make sure you have an idea of how big it is likely to get by running smaller tests if necessary.

 Use `Devel::DProf` to profile programs for bottlenecks.

11.3 Making Things Better

Here we discuss a few ways of improving your program's use of resources. You'll find terse descriptions of many more in *Programming Perl* (Chapter 8 in the second edition, Chapter 24 in the third).

11.3.1 Improving Execution Speed

It is common for improvements in execution speed to cost dearly in the readability department. Adding lookup caches, rearranging statement order, and inlining subroutine calls conspire to make a program less maintainable; therefore, as we have said before, you do these things only when you have to.

Once you've identified the code that is taking the most time, the next step is to optimize that code. A few suggestions follow.

 Inside a loop, take every opportunity to get out of it as early as possible.

I was just now writing some code to parse a log file containing lines like

```
20010208001507:POP3-Server:[198.137.241.43]:gwbush
```

The first statement in the loop was:

```
next unless my ($year, $month, $day, $hour, $minute,
                $second, $user)
  = /(\d\d\d\d) (\d\d) (\d\d) (\d\d) (\d\d) (\d\d):POP3-Server:.
*:(.*)/;
```

This may have been a natural translation of the obvious solution, but it was a tad slow on a 3 million line log file! Since many input lines did not match this pattern, I was able to speed up the elimination of those lines by inserting the following line of code at the beginning of the loop:

```
next unless index ($_, ':POP3-Server:') > 0;
```

(but not before making the mistake of leaving the parentheses out—can you see why that was wrong?).

This works because the string `:POP3-Server:` still uniquely identifies the lines we want. We can do more; in general, simple string operations work faster than regular expressions, so we can follow that line of code with these statements instead of the one that originally began the loop:

```
my ($year, $month, $day, $hour, $minute, $second)
  = unpack "A4A2A2A2A2A2", $line;
my ($user) = $line =~ /:POP3-Server:.*:(.*)/;
```

However, this benchmarks no faster than the previous code. We can use one more piece of information about the line to get an improvement: the last characters before the username are `]:`, and they don't occur anywhere else on the line. Benchmarking this code shows a speed increase of 50% over the alternative:

```
use Benchmark;
$line = <DATA>;
timethese (200000,
    {
    'unpack' => q{
       my ($year, $month, $day, $hour, $minute, $second)
          = unpack "A4A2A2A2A2A2", $line;
       my $user = substr $line, index ($line, ']:')+2;
       },
    'regex' => q{
       my ($year   , $month , $day, $hour,
           $minute, $second, $user)
          = ($line =~
/(\d\d\d\d)(\d\d)(\d\d)(\d\d)(\d\d)(\d\d):POP3-Server:.*:(.*)/
           );
    }
   });
__END__
20010208001507:POP3-Server:[198.137.241.43]:gwbush

Benchmark: timing 200000 iterations of regex, unpack...
    regex: 15 wallclock secs (15.63 usr +  0.02 sys =
                             15.65 CPU)
   unpack: 10 wallclock secs (10.42 usr +  0.00 sys =
                             10.42 CPU)
```

38 **Memoize function calls with common arguments.**

Using the CPAN module Memoize (http://search.cpan.org/
search?dist=Memoize) by Mark-Jason Dominus to transparently
remember the results of any function call gives you an easy way to trade memory for speed. You could do the same thing with slightly less execution overhead in your program by creating appropriate data structures and checking for the existence of an entry there before calling a function, but Memoize allows you to swap this capability in and out at the cost of a single line, and it can even save the results to disk to make them persistent.

We can illustrate this with an example that looks up the canonical Internet host name for various servers. It might be quite common to call `gethost-byname` for the same input more than once in, for instance, an application processing log files, and it's reasonable to assume that within a short period—say, a few minutes—the results won't change. Here's a benchmark:

```
use Benchmark;
use Memoize;

sub get_host_info
    {
      (gethostbyname shift) [0] || 'undefined';
    }

sub get_hosts
    {
    for (1..shift)
        {
          my $true_name = get_host_info "www.$_.com"
                          for 'aaa' .. 'abc';
        }
    }

get_hosts(1);    # Prime the local cache

timethese (4,
    {
    bare => q{ get_hosts(10) },
    memo => q{ use Memoize;
               memoize q(get_host_info); get_hosts(10) }
    });
```

For benchmark comparison purposes only, we first do a lookup on all the hosts so that the local nameserver has a chance to put the information in its cache. That stops the second benchmark from having an unfair advantage. Then we look up the host information for several hosts 10 times each. The results are:

```
timing 4 iterations of bare, memo...
      bare: 533 wallclock secs ( 0.70 usr +  0.65 sys =
                                1.35 CPU)
      memo: 11 wallclock secs ( 0.28 usr +  0.01 sys =
                                0.29 CPU)
     (warning: too few iterations for a reliable count)
```

Four iterations is just enough to smooth out any discrepancies caused by random fluctuations, but the `memoized` chunk still executes fast enough to cause `Benchmark` to warn us. In this case, the point has been already made.

39 Do everything possible in Perl rather than calling external programs.

Calling out to an external program may be *de rigueur* in shell scripts, but it costs time (spawning another process) that you often don't need to expend in a Perl script. There is no need to call `awk`, `sed`, `cut`, `head`, `grep`, or similar text filters unless you're not under time pressure and it happens to read better.

Be aware of where the dividing line lies, though. While you *can* use modules to send e-mail for you, opening a pipe to a mail program that takes care of queuing it is likely to be both faster and easier to read.

11.3.2 Improving Memory Usage

Just as the main CPU performance improvements are found in loops, the main memory gains are found in large data structures, so focus on how big your arrays and hashes get. Don't try to economize by using scalars to save the data instead; that takes up even more space because of the overhead attached to any variable in Perl. Prefer hashes to scalars and arrays to hashes; here's why:

```perl
#!/usr/bin/perl -wl
sub procsize
    {
    (split /\s+/, `ps -lp $$ | tail -1`)[9];
    # May not be 9 on your system
```

```
    }
sub randstring { join '', map chr rand 255, 1..100 }

my $base = procsize();

eval "\$$_ = randstring" for 'aaa' .. 'zzz';
print "Scalars: ", procsize() - $base;  $base = procsize;

$hash{$_} = randstring   for 'aaa' .. 'zzz';
print "Hash   : ", procsize() - $base;  $base = procsize;

push @array, randstring  for 'aaa' .. 'zzz';
print "Array  : ", procsize() - $base;
```

First we create a large number of scalars, each holding a random 100-character string. Then we create a hash with three-character keys and the same number and lengths of values, and populate an array similarly. After each step, we measure how much our process size has grown by looking at what ps prints in the SZ column. (It may be in a different column on your system; on non-Unix boxes you'll need to use whatever support your OS gives for measuring process size.) The output we got was

```
Scalars: 1749
Hash   : 682
Array  : 592
```

Packing multiple values in a scalar avoids the overhead of creating a new one. So instead of

```
push @array, $value;
#...
foreach $element (@array) { ... }
```

you can do

```
$scalar .= "$separator$value";
#...
while (($element) = $scalar =~ s/(.*?)($separator|$)//o)
   { ... }
```

   (Or, if speed is an issue, cook up something a little wordier using `substr` and `index`. If you were forming many small arrays, then you can just turn each one into a scalar that you `split` on `$separator` one at a time.) This is a last-ditch optimization that costs dearly in readability; comment the heck out of it if you have to use it.

 ## 40 Don't form unnecessary lists.

Some operations generate large lists when all you want to do is go through the elements one at a time. Structured data can usually be parsed a line at a time:

```
while (<INPUT>) { ... }
```

rather than reading the whole file:

```
{
local $/;
$file = <INPUT>;
}
```

   Although in the case of data that's not structured by lines, that may really be your best choice. The worst of both worlds would be to use the wrong loop statement:

```
for my $line (<INPUT>) { ... }
```

because that would read *all* the lines of the file into a list and then iterate through them one at a time.

   If you look at that example with scorn, thinking, "But *I* would never do *that*," then how about this?

```
for my $file (grep !/^\.\.?$/, readdir DIR) { ... }
```

Looks like an innocent enough standard idiom, and indeed it's quite safe, as long as you don't have any directories containing a humongous number of entries. But if you do, be aware that it requires temporary storage for a list nearly twice the size of those entries. If you'd like to bulletproof the code against that contingency, try this:

```
while (defined (my $file = readdir DIR))
    {
    next if $file =~ /^\.\.?$/;
    ...
    }
```

If you have very large hashes, consider `tie`ing them to a database to trade memory for speed and disk space:

```
use DB_File;         # There are several alternatives to this
my %large_hash;
tie %large_hash,     # The hash to tie
    'DB_File',       # The type of database to use
    'database';      # The file to store the database in
# use %large_hash...
untie %large_hash;   # Close the database file
```

However, you could easily abnegate your savings by using a common idiom:

```
for my $key (keys %large_hash) { ... }   # wrong!
```

because this will cause Perl to form in memory the list of all the keys. Use `each` instead, because it returns only two things at a time (or one, in scalar context):

```
while (my ($key, $value) = each %large_hash) { ... }
```

(Although you can't add or delete hash elements inside the loop.) If your hash values contain references (your hash keys can't, unless you're using the `Tie::RefHash` module), then you should use Gurusamy Sarathy's MLDBM (MultiLevel Database) module from CPAN (`http://search.cpan. org/search?dist=MLDBM`). Otherwise, the referents to which your references refer will not get stored in the database.

Avoid unnecessary copying.

Perl loves to copy data around. When you write a subroutine, say

```
sub bake
   {
   my ($temperature, $how_long) = @_;
   [...]
```

It's convenient to think of its first line as a kind of prototype, but in fact it's copying data. You may need to rethink this approach when passing huge variables to a subroutine. Caveat: While it's fine to get your data directly from @_, be aware that @_ is an alias for your original arguments; be sure you don't modify any of them without documenting the action. Furthermore, named parameter passing works by copying @_ into a hash; you'll have to come up with another way to recognize nonpositional arguments.

Sean M. Burke points out another application of this principle:

> Once I wrote a program to do some pretty horrific data conversion on an idiosyncratic markup language. Now, line-at-a-time processing was right out—the notation was SGML-like, i.e., freeform with its white space. Most or all of the manipulation was of the form
>
> ```
> $lexicon =~ s{<subhead>(.*?)</subhead>}
>              {handle_subhead($1)}ieg;
> ```
>
> The problem was that $lexicon was quite large (250+ KB), and applying lots and lots and LOTS of such regex search and replace operations took forever! Why? Because all the modifications of a large scalar involved copying it each time. One day it occurred to me that no replacement operation involved crossing entry boundaries (i.e., record boundaries), so I changed the program to chop the lexicon into entries, and then applied the string replacements to each of those via a foreach. Since each

entry was only ~2KB, there was MUCH less painful swapping, so the program ran about 50 times faster!

11.3.3 Improving Disk Space Usage

 Avoid temporary files.

If your operating system supports pipes, use them. Even if your operating system doesn't support them, Perl on your system might; try it.[5]

   If one part of your program writes a temporary file for another part to read, you can change this to use a pipe instead, but only if you can get those two parts of your program to execute reasonably concurrently. Otherwise you'll fill up the pipe when you write to it, and your program will twiddle its virtual thumbs waiting for the pipe to be unclogged. (If you've ever needed a plumber on the weekend, you know the feeling.) If you've coded something like this, consider breaking it into two separate programs that can be run concurrently and piped together.

---

5. As of version 5.6.0, `fork` in Perl works on Windows.

Chapter 12

Perl as a Second Language

"Through the darkness of future past, the magician longs to see.

One chants out between two worlds, fire walk with me!"

BOB in Twin Peaks

Many people come to Perl after already learning one or more other computer languages. (It is debatable whether Perl is a good choice as a first language for a new computer programmer. In our opinion, it is not, and one should first learn a procedural language such as C and an object-oriented language such as Java if for no other reason than to experience that great relief that comes when you start programming in Perl.) For those of you whose strength lies in one of the languages listed in this chapter, here are tips specifically for you. There is already much good information in this respect in the `perltrap` manual page; we have not duplicated them here, but urge you to look them up. You will also find *Perl: The Programmer's Companion*, by Nigel Chapman (Wiley, 1998), to be a good introduction to Perl.

12.1 Tips for Everyman

You need to make certain adjustments when coming to Perl from more familiar languages:

- Variables begin with type-specifying punctuation characters[1] referred to by some as *sigils*. It's not quite the revenge of Hungarian notation—no `mblock *apmblkMessages[]` here, thank goodness. The hardest thing for a Perl beginner to assimilate is that while, for example, `@animals` is the name of an array, `$animals[14]` is the name of a particular element in it, and `@animals[2..7]` is the name of a slice of that array. Just remember the rule that when you're referring to exactly one thing, it's a scalar and therefore begins with a `$`, whereas multiple things are an array—sort of—and begin with an `@` sign.

---

1. Well, most of them. Filehandles don't, unless you create one in a scalar with `IO::FileHandle` or the new 5.6 feature or assign a typeglob alias. And you'd have a hard time telling the difference between an lvaluable subroutine and a variable.

- Function arguments don't have to be surrounded by parentheses. Putting them in won't hurt, but knowing when you can leave them out makes your program easier to read. (See "The Case of the Vanishing Parentheses" in Chapter 4.)

- Because Perl insists on conditional clauses being blocks, there is no "dangling else" problem.

12.2 Tips for the C Programmer

You no longer must declare all your variables at the beginning of a block before any executable code. In fact, declaring them as late as possible is good practice because it keeps statements that belong to the same functional element together.

Perl's scalar variables are not strongly typed. They can switch oyster-like between integers, floating point numbers, and strings according to your whim (although if you ever turn a reference into a string, you can't turn it back). Even when you assign an object of a specific class to one, nothing stops you from overwriting it with an object of another class or something that isn't even an object at all. Polymorphism at its best. There is (as of version 5.005) the capability to declare to the compiler that a scalar is an object belonging to a particular class (my Dog $spot), but even that is only a loose agreement that you can break any time you feel like it.[2] (It allows for compile-time checking of accesses to fields, which are one way of implementing instance data.)

Dynamic (i.e., nonlexical) variables have global scope unless qualified with a local statement. But you won't want to program in this BASIC style anyway; declare all variables as lexical, and the scoping rules are the same ones you're already used to.

---

2. As of press time, Damian Conway had mooted a module which *could* restrict a variable to a particular object class, but not even the name had been agreed on.

Your days of wondering whether your `frees` match your `mallocs` are over! It is very hard to create a memory leak accidentally in Perl. Whenever you see code like this

```
$soldier = make_warrior ('squaddie');
sub make_warrior
    {
    my $fighter;
    ...
    return $fighter;
    }
```

which would make your heart leap into your mouth in C, relax. In C terms, `$fighter` is being allocated from the heap, not from the stack, so it doesn't become vulnerable as soon as the stack frame for `make_warrior` is unwound. Furthermore, the space allocated to `$fighter` doesn't get freed as long as there is a reference to it, and `$soldier` is such a reference. As long as something needs the space, it remains allocated, and as soon as nothing needs it, it gets freed. This is what you're used to spending all that time agonizing about in C.

Functions don't need `()` after them if you have no arguments to supply them, but if you do this with functions of your own, then their definition (or a prototype declaration) should precede their use.

Although in C the expressions `a[i]` and `i[a]` are equivalent, the corresponding expressions in Perl are not. If you find this surprising, you may need more help than we can provide.

While Perl inherits many operators (and their precedence) from C and probably strives hardest to be accessible to the C programmer, it also strives to be as orthogonal as possible. For example, while Perl provides the same `&&` and `||` operators as C, they return their inputs instead of a Boolean value. In other words, `$a || $b` is `$a` if `$a` is true; otherwise it is `$b`. (The operators short-circuit the same way). In another example, Perl figures anything that could be an lvalue, should be, so a term containing the trinary (`?:`) operator is an lvalue if its left and right parts are lvalues. The `substr` function is an lvalue if the result of its first argument is modifiable. And as of version 5.6.0, you can even (in an experimental feature) create a function of your own that is an lvalue.

Although no `switch` statement exists in Perl, this hasn't stopped people from inventing several dozen ways of simulating one, the latest being `Switch.pm`, a module presented by Damian Conway at the fourth annual Perl Conference (`http://conference.perl.com/`). The reason there isn't a `switch` is that when you start implementing one, your average `switch` statement seems very limited when you consider the breadth of Perl's operators. Why should each case be just a simple test for equality? Why not be able to compare against a regular expression as well? (Even the Bourne shell manages that.) Why shut out the vast set of logical comparisons? Until `Switch.pm`, it appeared that nothing could be implemented that wouldn't look like a poor cousin to the rest of the language. (It now seems that some version of `Switch.pm` will be incorporated into the core Perl 6 language.)

Hierarchical data structures are thoroughly typeless (atypical?) in Perl; no more fiddling with `union` statements to traverse heterogeneous lists. Some-times, people are afraid this means that they must pedantically check the type of every element of a complex object themselves to make sure they don't dereference something incorrectly; that is, until they realize that they were probably the ones who constructed the object in the first place, and they can usually trust themselves.

Don't look for a counterpart to `struct` expecting that you'll use it nearly as much. If you want to achieve exactly the same effect (named members of a compound variable) you can do so with a reference to a hash (or an object); but in practice, most of the uses you'd have for those things aren't necessary. There's no need to write special code for linked lists (although there's a book that shows you how if you have some exotic need[3]); Perl's arrays grow on demand quite well enough. Most of the reasons to construct trees are taken care of by Perl's efficient algorithm for looking up elements in hashes. (Again, if

---

3. *Mastering Algorithms with Perl*, by Jon Orwant, Jarkko Hietaniemi and John Macdonald (O'Reilly, 1999).

you have a need that somehow manages to overwhelm this mechanism, the same book provides alternatives.)

Some of the system calls you're accustomed to look like they were taken behind the woodshed by the tool set and given a workover to extend their usefulness. Instead of taking just one file as argument, `chmod`, `chown`, and `unlink` all take a list of filenames as arguments instead of just one. Oddly enough, `mkdir` and `rmdir` do not take lists of directory names even though their command line counterparts do.

'`lint`' is spelled '`use strict`' and '`-w`' in Perl.

12.3 Tips for the FORTRAN Programmer

Perl code appears quite odd to a FORTRAN programer. FORTRAN uses ( ) (parentheses) exclusively for indices. An array element has the form `ARRELM(1)`, a matrix element has the form `MATELM(1,1)`, and a subroutine call takes the form `CALL ASUB ( VALUE1, VALUE2 )`, whereas Perl uses ( ) (parentheses), [ ] (brackets), and { } (braces) in various ways depending on data type and function. For instance, whereas `$a[$i]` refers to an element of an array, `$a{$i}` refers to a value in a hash. Forgetting the proper uses of these separators is a common error for the neophyte Perler experienced in FORTRAN.

If you use FORTRAN for its native handling of high-precision floating point numbers (and if you don't—what *are* you using it for?), then you'll find Perl's IEEE floating point too imprecise (just as if you were to program in C). You may find solace in the `PDL` module from CPAN or the `Math::BigFloat` module in the Perl core.

`COMMON` blocks are an evil way of passing around scads of global variables at the same time and are used far more often in FORTRAN than they should be. (If you want to define common constants used by many FORTRAN files, use a preprocessor; this isn't the '60s, you know.) The way to make available a set of constants that share some common theme in Perl is to put them into a module, using the Exporter, and then import them where you want them:

```
% cat myconsts.pm
package myconsts;
use Exporter;
@ISA = qw(Exporter);
@EXPORT_OK = qw(PI E);
use constant PI => 3.14159265;
use constant E  => 2.71828183;
1;  # Modules must return a true value

% cat mytest
#!/usr/local/bin/perl
use myconsts qw(PI E);
print "PI*E = ", PI * E, "\n";

% mytest
PI*E = 8.53973421775655
```

That's worth a Perl of Wisdom:

43 **Put common sets of constants in their own modules using the Exporter, and use the modules where needed.**

If you prefer to use EQUIVALENCE—well, it's time to break the habit. You can create aliases for the same variable in Perl, but it's rarely useful. The Alias module provides an easy way of doing this if you must. If you want to alias one variable to the storage space of many, or vice-versa, as you can with EQUIVALENCE, well, you can't. And you'll get no sympathy from us.

If you are a FORTRAN programmer who never uses, nor intends to use, EQUIVALENCE statements or COMMON blocks, good! God only knows the measure of misery and heartache that has been inflicted on humanity by these monstrosities.

12.4 Tips for the Shell Programmer

You and the C programmer are Perl's favorite children (assuming that by "shell" we are talking about the Unix variety; the DOS/NT command line interface is quite a different beast). You alone among the other newcomers think it's quite natural for scalar variables to start with $, and you just need to get used to the fact that the $ is there during assignment as well as during reference. It may have seemed stifling at first that calls to external programs had to be wrapped in `system()`, although you were right at home with the use of backticks (` `` `) to capture program output. But if you tried to compensate by using `Shell.pm` just to avoid those `system()` calls, try doing without. A shell script needs a low syntactical overhead for calling external programs because it can do so little itself; Perl can do so much that calls to other programs are much less frequent. Overcome the tendency to call those beloved programs like `cut`, `head`, `sed`, and yes, even `awk` for text filtering; once you've learned to do the same things in Perl, you will seldom feel the need to go back. If you try converting a shell script to Perl, you'll find this principle rearing its head as you repeatedly excise calls to utility programs.

A shell program is interpreted a line at a time, which means that you can have any old junk representing your thoughts to date on the future direction of your script, as long as it won't actually get as far as executing any of those statements. Perl requires that the whole script be syntactically correct before it tries executing any of it, which means that you can't even hide something in an `if (0) { ... }` block without making sure that it is syntactically correct. But you can achieve the effect you want by inserting a line consisting solely of __END__ and the rest of the program will be ignored. (Actually, it becomes available for your program to read through the filehandle `DATA` if you wish.)

Perl's quoting rules will be a welcome relief—no more fighting to determine the combination of ', ", and \ to get what you want. The simple rule is: Interpolation (the Perl term for what you call parameter substitution) is determined only by the type of the outermost quotes. For instance, if you want to pass a variable that may contain spaces to the `grep` program, just say

```
system "grep -s '$quote' @files";
```

and the double quoting around the whole command ensures that $quote and @files are interpolated. The former is decorated with single quotes, and the elements of the latter are space-separated by default, exactly what we want. What if you want to embed $quote between double quotes instead? Perl allows you to put a double quote in a double-quoted string by preceding it with a backslash, but there is a cooler solution using Perl's qq quoting operator, which allows you to choose a different delimiter and thereby eliminate the need to backwhack quotation marks:

```
system qq(grep -s "$quote" @files);
```

If $quote can contain absolutely any characters, however, and you don't want any of them to be interpreted as metacharacters either by the shell or by the grep command, you need to make sure that all of the potential trouble-makers are escaped, and Perl has a special escape sequence pair just for the job:

```
system "grep -s \Q$quote\E @files"
```

Extending this to handle the possibility of members of @files containing white space or metacharacters is left as an exercise for the reader.

Speaking of operators, Perl uses eq and ne for strings, and == and != for numbers, which you probably think is the wrong way around.

You'll be pleased to learn that the return code for the backticks and system command is stored in the familiar $?. However, that return code is not the one you're used to; it's the one that C programmers get from their system call, so shift it right by eight bits to get the code you want. (The bottom eight bits contain information most people aren't interested in, like whether the program core dumped or what signal interrupted it, at least on Unix.)

12.5 Tips for the C++ or Java Programmer

The object-oriented features of Perl may appear frighteningly sparse; in fact, they are the consequence of a careful design to avoid unnecessarily bloating the language. For instance, there is no `this` keyword for referring to the current object in a method; instead, it's passed as the first parameter, and you can pick your own name. Most people pick `$self` because the declaration `my $self`... has a nice ring to it (or because they are former Smalltalk programmers).

Run-time semantics alone determine whether a routine is an object method or a class method, so you can easily write one that swings both ways. (A common idiom makes an object method out of a constructor.)

There is nothing special about a constructor method in Perl; you can call it anything you want, but most Perl programmers call it `new` to make you feel welcome. Not only is the underlying implementation of an object exposed, but you get to implement it yourself from a bewildering array of choices. (The one you'll feel most comfortable with is a hash; don't even look at the others until you've gotten the hash under your belt.) And there is no native support for creating instance data attributes or inheriting them, although there are optional pragmata (`base`, `fields`) that provide some syntactical sugaring for doing so.

Regardless, your callers should not access your instance data directly but instead via accessor methods. You may use a module (such as `Class::Struct`) to create those methods automatically, although it seems that any class worth writing these days requires custom logic in each accessor method anyway.

It is possible for a caller to modify the object's instance data directly unless you go to great lengths to make the instance data as private as you're accustomed to. (See "Closures as Objects" in the `perltoot` documentation page.) This is rarely perceived as a problem in Perl since the philosophy is that people who fiddle with instance data directly when the specification for the public interface to the class doesn't permit it deserves whatever they get.

Because there are no function prototypes (of the kind you're used to) in Perl, there is no method overloading with different prototype signatures. You get to validate the number and type of arguments you're called with at run time, if you want.

You cannot enforce abstract (pure virtual) methods to be overridden at compile time, but you can create one that throws a run-time exception, unless it has been overridden.

You'll find more methodical comparisons among Perl, C++, and Java in Damian Conway's excellent book, *Object-Oriented Perl* (Manning, 1999).

12.5.1 Specific Tips for the Java Programmer

In Perl you have the option of creating a program that is not at all object-oriented and—horrors—isn't even a class. This is actually the best approach for solving many problems, as hard as it may be to get out of the habit of doing a class hierarchy decomposition every time you write a program.

The issue of "to what extent code you publish for reuse should be object-oriented" has engendered fiercely partisan arguments in the Perl community, with impassioned advocates at both ends of the spectrum. The upshot of this is that you can take whatever position you want and justify it by an appeal to authority.[4] Our rule of thumb is: If you're writing something just for your own use which is not likely to have significant reusability, the overhead for making it object-oriented is unlikely to be worthwhile. If you're writing something to be used by other people, an O-O interface will probably be worth the effort, considering how neatly it separates the interface from the implementation and relieves you of the need to provide any more support than simply ensuring that the interface lives up to its promises.

Garbage collection in Perl does not happen asynchronously, but is entirely deterministic (except for the order in which objects are freed during global

---

4. Use everything to your advantage...

destruction at the end of a program). When the reference count on an object drops to zero, it is destroyed immediately.

Although Java allows you to inherit from only one concrete base class and multiple abstract classes, Perl makes no distinction between the two kinds of class and says that you can do as much multiple inheritance as you like. You may find that your fears about incestuous inheritance relationships do not come to pass, however.

Reflection in Perl is accomplished by several methods. If the object `$obj` is implemented as a hash, you can discover its set of attributes with `keys %$obj`. You can find out if it supports a given method `meth` with `$obj->can('meth')`, and you can get a list of all the methods it supports by traversing the symbol table for the package looking for subroutines. Finally, you can construct its inheritance hierarchy by following the `@ISA` array package variable or by using the CPAN module `Class::ISA` (`http://search.cpan.org/search?dist=Class-ISA`) which provides a friendly interface for that.

Finalizer chaining does not happen automatically in Perl either—the Perl term for `finalize` is `DESTROY`—and for much the same reasons as in Java.

In keeping with the Perl philosophy of permissiveness, there is no equivalent of `final` to prevent a method from being overridden in a derived class.

12.5.2 Specific Tips for the C++ Programmer

The lack of strong typing which probably seemed liberating to the C programmer probably seems offensive to you. (Perl may seem irritatingly free-form until you grasp the Perl ethos.)

Perl does have operator overloading, although it isn't used as often as you'd think. `perldoc overload` tells you all about it.

Because Perl doesn't have strong typing, you won't need to construct template classes for generic operations since they're generic to begin with.

We personally find the use of references in C++ to be annoying, because a change in a function prototype can change the actual value that is passed in a call to the function. If you actually like this feature, you can replicate it—after a fashion—with what Perl calls *subroutine prototypes*. They won't look like prototypes to you—they're more like patterns specifying the order and types of arguments that can be passed—but one of the consequences is that you can construct a prototype that will allow a subroutine to be called with an array and receive a reference to that array where it would normally receive the list of all the elements in the array.

We suggest you not be too hasty to avail yourself of this feature, primarily because unlike C++, Perl does not require prototypes to be declared in order for a program to work, and if yours somehow fail to get declared—or get declared too late—then the semantics of your program will change in wonderfully unpredictable ways.

Chapter 13

Debugging CGI Programs

"Would you tell me, please, which way I ought to go from here?"

"That depends a good deal on where you want to get to," said the Cat.

Alice in Alice's Adventures in Wonderland *by Lewis Carroll*

The Cheshire Cat was renowned for oblique comments and a propensity to vanish partially or completely at inconvenient times. Running Common Gateway Interface (CGI) programs through a Web server can leave one feeling a lot like Alice (including stretched thin and squashed).

13.1 CGI

A glance at `comp.lang.perl.misc` reveals that many people don't understand the difference between the CGI protocol and the Perl scripts that use it. We therefore consider it our civic duty to take the time to explain it here, even though we're talking about something that is not Perl. (That's the Perl connection—that it has nothing to do with Perl. It's all very Gödel-like.)

The Common Gateway Interface is a specification for how a Web server can deliver dynamic content. It says that you can have a URL that points not to a static file but to a program whose output will be sent to the browser. The user of the browser cannot tell the difference between a CGI program and a static file by looking at what the server returns; the only clue is that the URL usually looks different. (Instead of ending in `.html`, it probably ends in `.cgi` or contains `/cgi-bin/`. There's nothing hard and fast about this rule though. It's easy to configure a Web server to return static pages whose URLs look like CGI programs, and vice-versa.) The point, however, is that they shouldn't care what produced the output.

The CGI specification spells out how a program invoked in this way can have inputs sent by a browser (as part of the URL using an HTTP GET command or in HTTP content with a POST command), how the program can see those inputs (in the `QUERY_STRING` environment variable or in their standard input respectively), how the inputs are encoded (a format that turns many characters into a hexadecimal representation), and what the program has to send in addition to the browser-visible content of its output (HTTP headers specifying the type of that content).

Nothing in the CGI specification specifies a particular language for CGI programs. This is why people who ask questions about CGI get attacked for asking them in a Perl newsgroup. The answer would be the same no matter what language the program was written in, and it wouldn't have anything to do with Perl. The newsgroup the attackers want those questions taken to is `comp.infosystems.www.authoring.cgi`.

So how can you tell whether your question or problem is Perl related or CGI related?

- If your program produces apparently correct output when run from the command line, but the Web browser displays a `500 - Server Error` message, it's a CGI problem. If you can't run the program from the command line on the Web server, see our tips that follow.

- If your program is not picking up form inputs and you're using `CGI.pm`, the Web server has a problem. Test it with our `cgi-test` program that follows. If you're not using `CGI.pm`, few people are likely to assist you because you're making the task unnecessarily difficult.

- If your program takes too long to produce any output, the browser will give up and display a "Document contained no data" message. You may need to use a nonparsed header (nph) script if your Web server otherwise buffers your output, or else figure out how to produce output before the browser times out.

See `http://hoohoo.ncsa.uiuc.edu/cgi/interface.html` for reference information on CGI.

13.2 Web Servers

There are many combinations of types and versions of Web servers, platforms and operating systems on the World Wide Web. Their differences in behavior are outside the scope of this book. We aim to make our advice applicable to the widest range of such combinations, but when we fail, unless otherwise noted, what we say has been tested against a recent version of Apache on Linux.

References on Apache:

- *Apache: The Definitive Guide*, 2nd edition, by Ben & Peter Laurie (O'Reilly, 1999)
- `http://www.apache.org/`

13.3 500—Server Error

The primal `ed` editor for Unix has one and only one response to any kind of error condition: it prints '?'.[1] Although user interface design has generally matured from this minimalist approach since then, it took a giant leap backwards with the introduction of Web servers whose only response to virtually any error is something close to

```
Internal Server Error

The server encountered an internal error or misconfiguration
and was unable to complete your request.
```

It usually goes on to suggest that you look in the server error log, but unfortunately it doesn't go to the trouble of including the part that might be relevant.

 If at all possible, get an interactive login on the Web server for which you are developing. If you can't, consider using a different service.

---

1. `ed` was written by Ken Thompson. It was suggested that his car sported a single indicator on the dashboard: a giant '?' which would light up when anything was wrong, and the experienced driver would usually know what it meant.

There are several reasons for this, starting with the fact that it is a lot easier to look at the error log file if we can look at it with programs like `tail` or `less` than if we have to view the whole thing through a Web page. If you can't get an interactive login, you may nevertheless be able to figure out where your Web server keeps its log files (the defaults are well known and commonly used) and you then can use a CGI program like the following to look at the last ten (say) lines:

```
#!/usr/bin/perl -Tw
use strict;
use CGI qw(:standard);
my $TAIL = 10;

print header, start_html;
my @lines;

# Change next line as needed
my $file = "/usr/local/apache/logs/error_log";
open (IN, $file) or die p(b("Unable to open $file: $!"));

while (<IN>)
    {
    push @lines, $_;
    shift @lines if @lines > $TAIL;
    }

print p("Total number of lines = $.\nLast $TAIL lines:\n");
close IN;
print pre(@lines), end_html;
```

Little tools like this populate the black bag carried by CGI programmers from job to job. In fact, if you can't even get Perl working on a (Unix) site that you can't log in to, here's a Bourne shell version:

```
#!/usr/bin/sh
LOG=/var/log/httpd/error_log
TAIL=10
echo "Content-type: text/plain"
echo
echo "Total number of lines = `wc -l $LOG`"
echo
tail -$TAIL $LOG
```

13.4 Basics

To avoid those "Doh!" moments, make sure that

- Your program has the execute bit set on Unix systems. The pen-
  alty for missing this one is a 403 Forbidden error, which is
  likely to make you think that the Web server can't get into the
  enclosing directory instead.
- Your program has the correct #! line at the beginning. Getting it
  wrong will earn you a 500 Server Error.

Both of these problems are instantly detected by running the program from
the command line on the Web server itself. If that works but you still get an
error when coming through a Web browser, the permissions for the Web server
user are set up incorrectly; contact the Web server administrator.

13.5 Security

Not long ago, security was still considered optional by many people. Today
that attitude is widely recognized as dangerous to others as well as oneself.
The issue of security on the Internet has garnered universal attention, and one
of the ways a host can be broken into is through a poorly written CGI program.

Don't let yours be one of them.

13.5.1 Taint mode

Perl provides a powerful mechanism for securing your CGI programs. It's called *taint mode*, and no program you put on the Web should be without it. You invoke it with the -T flag, making the first line of your scripts

```
#!/usr/bin/perl -wT
```

(Of course, the path to your `perl` may change.)

Taint mode doesn't actually do anything by itself to secure your program. What it does is force you to address every place where a security hole could occur. You see, the chief cause of security holes in CGI programs is malicious user inputs being used to affect things outside of your program. If you've never seen how easy this is, you're in for a shock.

Let's say that your e-commerce Web site contains a feedback form for a user to input their e-mail address and a message of praise. Unfortunately, let's say that your shipping department sent a customer a Barbie doll instead of the Sony PlayStation he ordered, and rather than praise, this soon-to-be-former customer has a different message for you. In the e-mail address field, he types `` `rm * ` ``. Your script, after reading the user input into a variable `$email`, reasonably enough sends a response:

```
open MAIL, "|$SENDMAIL $email" or die $!;
```

(We'll talk about better ways of signaling errors shortly.) Net result: Chaos. If you're running on DOS instead, don't think you're safe; that user could have entered `; erase *.*`. What you need to do is check the e-mail address that's been entered and make sure it won't cause that kind of problem. Now, suppose we assume for a moment that valid e-mail addresses match the pattern

```
\w[\w*%.:-]*@\w[\w.-]*\w
```

(That's not quite true, but it'll do for our example.) After setting `$email` from the user input, we could massage it:

```
($email) = $email =~ /(\w[\w*%.:-]*@\w[\w.-]*\w)/;
unless ($email)
  {
  # Code to handle no valid email being entered
  }
```

From the user's input, we extracted an e-mail address that won't cause any nasty side effects when passed to our mail program. If we don't find anything in the input matching that, we can treat it as if nothing at all was entered.

You might also choose to compare the result of the match with what they entered, and if they differ, grumble about a "nonstandard" address being entered. Before you use that language, however, consider this caveat: the preceding pattern is a grossly simplified version of what it really takes to match a valid e-mail address. The RFC 822 standard (`http://www.ietf.org/rfc/rfc0822.txt`) specifies a complicated syntax that includes several ways of embedding comments that are arguably not part of the address at all and unlikely to be entered by a user in a Web form. A regular expression to match it is more than 6K in length and is the *tour de force* conclusion of Jeffrey Friedl's seminal book, *Mastering Regular Expressions* (O'Reilly, 1997). A slighly shorter and somewhat more practical approach is contained in Chapter 9 of the second edition of *CGI Programmming with Perl* by Scott Guelich, Shishir Gundavaram, and Gunther Birznieks (O'Reilly, 2000), but even this book acknowledges that its algorithm's value is principally instructional. (It doesn't confirm that the address can receive e-mail; only an attempt to send mail there can do that.)

What taint mode does is force you to launder input data as we just described. Any data that comes from outside your program—including even environment variables or directory listings—has associated with it a special flag that marks it as *tainted*. Any attempt to use tainted data to affect something outside of your program—such as input to an external program—results in a run-time exception before that can happen. (The error will mention an "insecure dependency.") And if you use a tainted variable in an expression that is assigned to another variable, that variable becomes tainted too.

The *only* way to derive untainted data from tainted data is to perform a regular expression match with capturing parentheses on it and use the resulting $1, $2, etc. It is assumed that if you have gone to this much trouble, you have constructed a regular expression that will result in safe data. Perl *does not*—and *cannot*—check that you have really done so. If you simply do

```
($untainted) = $tainted =~ /(.*)/s;
```

then this is the equivalent of putting a gun to your head and pulling the trigger without looking in the chamber first.

 Create CGI programs with taint checking from the beginning. Retrofitting -T onto existing programs is tedious and frustrating.

Taint mode is utterly paranoid. One of the consequences of environment variables being tainted is that your path is tainted, so any attempt to run an external program fails with an `insecure dependency in path` unless you untaint `$ENV{PATH}`, which usually means setting it explicitly to a (colon- or semicolon-separated) list of directories you trust.

13.5.2 Debugging in Taint Mode

If you syntax check a program that has -T in its #! line, you'll see something like this:

```
$ perl -c foo.cgi
Too late for "-T" option at foo.cgi line 1.
```

This is caused by an obscure feature of Perl's implementation that requires taint mode to be turned on really early in its startup process. (If you remembered Perl of Wisdom #10—Use `use diagnostics` to explain error messages—you would have seen the explanation.) Just add -T:

```
$ perl -cT foo.cgi
```

13.6 Heading Off Errors

The output of your program is usually parsed through the Web server (unless you use the increasingly rare nph feature), which adds headers like a status line (unless you provide one yourself), a server identification line, and a date. The essential header for you to remember is `Content-type`: you must output this one.

(Weeell...the complete truth is more complicated, but of little use. You can output any number of lines that look like headers [any line containing a colon with at least one nonspace character on either side, based on experimentation], and these lines are faithfully passed on by the server as though they actually mean something. As long as you output a blank line before your content, it'll make it through; if you don't output a `Content-type` header, some servers will put one on for you [set to `text/plain`]; some browsers interpret the absence of a `Content-type` header to mean it is of type `text/html`. This is of academic interest at best.)

The bottom line is that the first output from your program must be header lines including a `Content-type` header, which must be followed by a blank line before your content. If you use `CGI.pm`, the `header` routine is all you need to output headers properly; as long as you call it before anything else that produces output, you should have little to worry about. But sometimes, the bugs can gang up on you and foil this strategy.

 Run your CGI program from the command line to check that it produces the right output in the right order.

It is crucial to find out what your program outputs to STDERR. This is where the output from `die` and `warn` goes, including any complaints from `use strict` or `-w`. The popular Apache server puts STDERR messages in the error log file, but the Netscape Enterprise server directs them to the browser in the order it receives them. What will that be? Let's look at a simple script that produces a warning in addition to output:

```
#!/usr/bin/perl -w
use strict;
my $x;
print "Content-type: text/plain\n\n";
print "Value of \$x is $x\n";
```

Run this at the shell prompt and you'll see

```
Content-type: text/html

Use of uninitialized value in concatenation (.) at foo.cgi line
5.
Value of $x is
```

But that's not the order the output goes to the Web server! Because we're outputting to the terminal, STDOUT is by default *line buffered*, which means that its output is flushed on every newline. However, if output is not going to the terminal, STDOUT is *fully buffered* (unless the Web server decides otherwise), and won't come out until *after* the output to STDERR.

Upshot: try this on a server that sends STDERR to the browser as well, and you'll get a `500 Server Error`. As far as the server was concerned, you sent

```
Use of uninitialized value in concatenation (.) at foo.cgi line
5.
Content-type: text/html

Value of $x is
```

The first line does not look like a header.

Whew! Is this a lot to remember or what? That's why we reiterate: Test your program from the command line first and follow Perl of Wisdom #17—Eliminate all warnings before proceeding with development. In addition, add the line

```
$| = 1;
```

near the beginning of your program to unbuffer STDOUT so that when you
send output, it gets passed to the Web server immediately.

13.7 cgi-test

Let's add to our black bag the following script:

```
#!/usr/bin/perl -Tw
use strict;
print "Content-type: text/plain\n\n";
print "$_: $ENV{$_}\n" for sort keys %ENV;
print "\nInput:\n";
print <STDIN>;
```

Use this whenever you have doubts about what a form is really sending to
the server. Just make this script the target of the form action, and you'll get a
terse dump of the environment variables and any content that the form sent via
POST.

13.8 Eavesdropping

Sometimes you'd just like to listen in on the conversation between a browser
and a server, like a gossip-hungry neighbor on a party line. Perhaps you're
dealing with browsers whose caching behavior is questionable, and you don't
want to guess what's really being fetched. You could use a connection-sniffing
tool like tcpdump to monitor the traffic between the client and the server, but
this generally requires superuser access to put the network interface into "pro-
miscuous" mode. So try instead our proxylog tool:

```
#!/usr/bin/perl -w
use strict;

use Getopt::Std;
use IO::Socket;
```

```perl
use IO::Select;

sub usage
    {
    <<"EndUsage";
$0 lets you snoop on the conversation between a client
and server.

$0 -i clientport -o serverhost:port [-1] [-v]
        -i      incoming port to listen to
        -o      outgoing port to make connection to
        -1      only process one client request, then exit
        -v      verbose

Caveats:
    o  Does not handle multiple simultaneous connections.
    o  Reads are asynchronous, writes are synchronous.
    o  Messages larger than 64K will be segmented.
EndUsage
    }

use vars qw($opt_i $opt_o $opt_1 $opt_v);
getopts('i:o:1:v') and $opt_o or die usage;
my $proxy_port = $opt_i or die usage;
my ($server_host, $server_port) = $opt_o =~ /^(.+):(\d+)$/
    or die usage;
my $verbose  = 1 if $opt_v;
my $only_one = 1 if $opt_1;

$SIG{TERM} = $SIG{INT} = $SIG{HUP} = \&shutdown;

my $proxy = IO::Socket::INET->new(LocalPort => $proxy_port,
                                  Type      => SOCK_STREAM,
                                  Proto     => 'tcp',
                                  Reuse     => 1,
                                  Listen    => 1)
    or die "Can't listen on port $proxy_port: $!\n";
print "[listening on port $proxy_port]\n" if $verbose;

my ($client, $server);

OUTER:
```

```
while ($client = $proxy->accept)
   {
   my ($client_host, $client_port) =
          (gethostbyaddr($client->peeraddr, AF_INET)
            || $client->peerhost,
           $client->peerport);
   print "[connection from $client_host on $client_port]\n"
       if $verbose;

   $server = IO::Socket::INET->new(PeerAddr => $server_host,
                                   PeerPort => $server_port,
                                   Proto    => 'tcp',
                                   Type     => SOCK_STREAM)
       or die "Can't connect to $server_host:$server_port\n";
   print "[connected to server $server_host:$server_port]\n"
       if $verbose;

   my $selector = IO::Select->new($client, $server);

CONNECTION:
   while (my @ready = $selector->can_read)
      {
      for my $sock (@ready)
         {
         my ($who, $target) = ($sock == $client
                                  ? ('client', $server)
                                  : ('server', $client));
         my $msgbuf;
         unless ($sock->sysread($msgbuf, 64 * 1024))
             {
             print "[$who closed connection]\n" if $verbose;
             last CONNECTION;
             }
         (my $safebuf = $msgbuf) =~
             tr/\011\012\015\040-\176\240-\376/./cs;
         print "\n===== \U$who\E:\n$safebuf";
         print "\n" unless substr($safebuf, -1, 1) eq "\n";
         $target->syswrite($msgbuf, length $msgbuf);
         }
      last OUTER if $only_one;
      }
   print "[closing connection]\n" if $verbose;
```

```
    $client->shutdown(2) if $client;
    $server->shutdown(2) if $server;
    }

sub shutdown
    {
    print "[shutting down]\n" if $verbose;
    $client->shutdown(2) if $client;
    $server->shutdown(2) if $server;
    $proxy ->shutdown(2);
    exit(0);
    }
```

Let's say that you want to see exactly what travels between the browser and
server when you visit a URL like `http://webhost/path/file.html`.
Run this script like so:

% **proxylog -i 2222 -o webhost:80**

Now the script is listening on port 2222. (You can pick any number you like—
on a Unix system you need to be root to pick anything below 1024—but you
want to avoid the numbers for any well-known services your computer might
already use.)[2] Let's say that the machine on which you run `proxylog` is
called *listener*.[3]   Enter   the   URL   `http://listener:2222/path/`
`file.html` into your browser, and watch the transaction be printed out by
`proxylog`:

```
===== CLIENT:
GET / HTTP/1.0
Connection: Keep-Alive
User-Agent: Mozilla/4.72 [en] (Win98; I)
Pragma: no-cache
Host: 204.179.152.52:2222
Accept: image/gif, image/x-xbitmap, image/jpeg, image/pjpeg,
image/png, */*
```

---

2. Like, for instance, 6667 (IRC), or 6699 (Napster).

3. We've omitted domains like `.com` from the host names here, but you may need them when you run
    `proxylog`.

```
Accept-Encoding: gzip
Accept-Language: en
Accept-Charset: iso-8859-1,*,utf-8


===== SERVER:
HTTP/1.1 200 OK
Date: Tue, 01 Aug 2000 19:54:37 GMT
Server: Apache/1.3.12 (Unix)  (Red Hat/Linux) PHP/3.0.15
mod_perl/1.21
Last-Modified: Wed, 01 Mar 2000 18:37:44 GMT
ETag: "32ae2-9cf-38bd6378"
Accept-Ranges: bytes
Content-Length: 2511
Keep-Alive: timeout=15, max=100
Connection: Keep-Alive
Content-Type: text/html

<!DOCTYPE HTML PUBLIC "-//W3C//DTD HTML 3.2 Final//EN">
[...]
```

Any anchors or embedded URLs (such as images) that do not specify the Web server will also go through `proxylog` when they are fetched.[4]

13.9 CGI.pm

We've mentioned `CGI.pm` several times, but now it's time to address it in more depth. This module provides a functional interface to generating HTML,[5] an object-oriented or functional interface to processing form inputs, and functions for supporting every other conceivable operation associated with user interaction through CGI. If you're concerned about performance—taking into account Perl of Wisdom #33—then you'll want to look into options like `mod_perl`, `FastCGI`, and `CGI::Lite`. These are outside the scope of this book, here are some references to them:

---

4. `proxylog` can be downloaded from `www.perldebugged.com`.

5. And even makes it XHTML-compliant in recent versions.

- *Writing Apache Modules with Perl and C: The Apache API and mod_perl*, by Lincoln Stein and Doug MacEachern (O'Reilly, 1999)
- *Writing CGI Applications with Perl,* by Kevin Meltzer and Brent Michalski (Addison-Wesley, 2001)
- `http://www.fastcgi.com/`
- `http://search.cpan.org/search?dist= CGI-Lite`

Writing code to handle the CGI protocol is harder than it looks; writing it yourself instead of using `CGI.pm` is like making whipped cream with a fork while a shiny electric mixer stands idly by.[6] We will just touch on the debugging issues here; for comprehensive documentation on `CGI.pm` check out:

- *Official Guide to Programming with CGI.pm*, by Lincoln Stein (Wiley, 1998)
- *CGI Programming with Perl*, 2nd ed., by Scott Guelich, Shishir Gundavaram, and Gunther Birznieks (O'Reilly, 2000)

If anyone is going to inspect the HTML generated by a CGI.pm program—either for command line debugging or for viewing the source from a Web browser—you may want to change the `use CGI` statement to `use CGI::Pretty`. This will insert line breaks and indentation to create, well, pretty output.

13.10 Command Line Testing

A `CGI.pm` program is easily tested from the command line; as soon as the program calls a CGI method or creates a CGI object it will prompt

```
(offline mode: enter name=value pairs on standard input)
```

---

6. It can be done, but it's murder on the elbows.

and you can then type a series of lines like:

```
address="742 Evergreen Terrace"
phone=555-8707
```

End them with whatever character signals end-of-input to your current shell. The inputs you cannot provide this way are

- File uploads.
- Cookies: You can pass them by setting the environment variable HTTP_COOKIE to the name of the cookie followed by an = sign and the value of the cookie.
- User authentication: Set the REMOTE_USER environment variable to the name of the authenticated user. A Web server will not pass the password the user typed to your program anyway.

If your program does something different when you run it from the command line than when you run it through a browser, here are the things to check:

- Path: These are probably different. Set $ENV{PATH} explicitly in your program to satisfy taint mode, and set it the same way in your command shell.
- Current directory: The Web server may set this to something other than the directory the program is located in. Use absolute paths for filenames for input and output, or chdir to absolute paths first.
- Cookies: Try disabling these in your browser to see if it makes a difference, or use something like our proxylog tool to see what cookie transactions take place over the Web.
- Permissions and ownerships: Does your program read any files that are inaccessible to the UID the Web server process runs under? Does your program modify any files outside of scratch directories? If so, bear in mind that the Web server process UID has very little authority (hopefully). You'll need to give write permission to that UID for anything like this.

• Environment: There may be some environment variable set only in your command line shell (like LD_LIBRARY_PATH) that modifies the behavior of programs executed by your program. Compare all your environment variables with the ones reported by cgi-test.

13.11 Dying Young

Perhaps the most vexing problem to deal with in CGI programming is how to handle exceptions. If something in your program dies, it (normally) prints a message to STDERR and exits. The error message doesn't look like an HTTP header, so if it comes out before you get to print the headers you'll get a 500 Server Error. And if it comes out later, it won't be in HTML (or GIF, or whatever you're outputting) and will mess up the formatting of what you're in the middle of sending.

This is mostly addressed by the CGI::Carp module. With the statement use CGI::Carp qw(fatalsToBrowser); if your program ever dies, the message will be trapped and output to the browser.[7] So, to use a short example, consider the following CGI program:

```perl
#!/usr/bin/perl -w

use strict;
use CGI qw(:standard);
use CGI::Carp qw(fatalsToBrowser);

my ($num_angels, $pinhead_size) = (1_000_000_000, 0);

print header, start_html, h1('Philosophy 101');

print p(<<"EOP");
```

---

7. If you leave out the fatalsToBrowser parameter, then output to STDERR gets identified and timestamped. This is healthy when you're using a server that sends that to the error log—you can tell what generated each message and when.

```
Other Web sites wonder how many angels can dance on the
head of a pin; we calculate it for you.
EOP

print p('The answer is ', $num_angels/$pinhead_size);
print end_html;
```

This will produce something like:

> **Philosophy 101**
> Other Web sites wonder how many angels can dance on the
> head of a pin; we calculate it for you.
> Content-type: text/html
> Software error:
> Illegal division by zero at /home/peter/
> public_html/foo.cgi line 12.
> For help, please send mail to the webmaster.

This doesn't do you much good if your program is outputting an image and has already sent the header, but fortunately the vast majority of CGI programs output HTML.

In production code, it is inadvisable to reveal error messages to end users for reasons of aesthetics and security. Randal Schwartz recently released a *Linux Magazine* column on a module called `FatalsToEmail` that e-mails errors to developers; see `http://www.stonehenge.com/merlyn/LinuxMag/col14.html`. See also Jonas Liljegren's CPAN module `CGI::Debug` at `http://search.cpan.org/search?dist=CGI-Debug` for some error reporting and tracing features.

13.12 Debugger Interaction

If you execute a CGI program that uses `fatalsToBrowser` under the debugger, you may see a screenful of ugly (but benign) output like:

```
<H1>Software error:</H1>
<CODE>Can't locate Term/ReadLine/Gnu.pm in @INC
```

The reason for this is one of the more cobwebby areas of Perl. The Perl interactive debugger[8] loads the `Term::ReadLine` module, which contains the lines

```
eval "use Term::ReadLine::Gnu; 1"
  or eval "use Term::ReadLine::Perl; 1";
```

This is a quite reasonable way to load `Term::ReadLine::Gnu` if it exists, and to load `Term::ReadLine::Perl` if it doesn't. Unfortunately, the `$SIG{__DIE__}` handler (see section 9.4) installed by `CGI::Carp` gets called first when something dies. Even if another mechanism to catch an exception has been put in place, that mechanism won't get to look at it. If you want to see the effects of this for yourself, try this program:

```
#!/usr/bin/perl -w
use strict;
BEGIN { $SIG{__DIE__} = sub { print "Arrgh: @_" } }
eval { my $x = 1 / @ARGV };
print "Caught exception: $@";
```

The reason we divide by `@ARGV` and not `0` is that the optimizer performs the division at compile time if it can, and this would obscure the point we're trying to make. The program prints

```
Arrgh: Illegal division by zero at line 4.
Caught exception: Illegal division by zero at line 4.
```

It's entirely possible (read: desirable) that this behavior will change in a future version of Perl. In the meantime, if you want to avoid the spew upon starting the debugger, you can safely replace

```
use CGI::Carp qw(fatalsToBrowser);
```

---

8. In the file `perl5db.pl`, if you're curious.

with the following:

```
BEGIN
    {
    unless (exists $DB::{DB})
        {
        require CGI::Carp;
        import CGI::Carp qw(fatalsToBrowser);
        }
    }
```

13.12.1 Taint Misbehavin'

If you attempt to run a program that has taint checking turned on under the debugger, nasty things will happen when you try to examine or change data at the debugger prompt. This should be fixed in the 5.6.1 release of Perl; if it isn't (or you can't wait), and you need to interactively debug scripts you can't or don't want to remove a -T flag from, you'll have to find the file perl5db.pl and patch it to insert the line shown in bold below that should be at or near line 1510:

```
local $otrace  = $trace;
local $osingle = $single;
local $od      = $^D;

{ ($evalarg) = $evalarg =~ /(.*)/s;  }

@res    = eval "$usercontext $evalarg;\n";  # '\n' for nice \
recursive debug
$trace  = $otrace;
$single = $osingle;
```

13.13 ptkdb

The ptkdb debugger (see Chapter 7) has a way for you to debug CGI programs as they run on the server, which is as close as it comes to having your cake and eating it too. The following conditions must be met:

- The server has to have Tk, PerlTk, and ptkdb installed.

- The debug client has to be running an X Window System server. This machine doesn't have to be the same as the one running the browser making the request, however.

- The environment variable PTKDB_DISPLAY on the server has to be set to the X display of the debug client.

- You have to be able to accomplish your debugging without interrupting the flow of output long enough for the browser to time out. After that time, you may be able to continue debugging the program, but you won't see what it outputs.

Because PTKDB_DISPLAY has to be set very early in the program invocation, it is no good setting it in %ENV or even in a BEGIN block. The easiest way to circumvent this is to wrap your Perl program in a shell script, like so:

```
#!/bin/sh
PTKDB_DISPLAY=client.perldebugged.com:0
export PTKDB_DISPLAY
/usr/bin/perl -Twd:ptkdb <<\END_OF_CGI_PROGRAM

Perl CGI program appears here

END_OF_CGI_PROGRAM
```

Note that we had to include the -T and -d options when we ran perl. Leaving them to the #! line doesn't work.

 A final note: Never trust a Cheshire cat to do what you expect.

Chapter 14

Conclusion

> "You can never entirely stop being what you once were.
> That's why it's important to be the right person today,
> and not put it off till tomorrow."
> Larry Wall, Creator of Perl

14.1 Finis

Do not assume the techniques and tips described in this book represent the mythical "correct way to debug." Such a thing does not exist any more than does the "right way to program." The aim was not to tell you how to debug, rather to demonstrate the procedures we (the authors) use to debug (successfully, for the most part).

14.2 The End

We close by expanding on a theme from Chapter 2. When we asked ourselves why some people work on their skills, exercise their curiosity, and try new things whereas others don't, the bottom line has to do with love. The reason people work constantly on improving Perl, with no direct compensation, is simply that they love programming and they love Perl.

More than any other language, Perl inspires this dedication because of the way its design embodies the principles that programming should be fun and the language should do what you want. Perl is a fun language.[1] Fun to use, to learn, and to improve. As we said in Chapter 1, a relative amateur can use Perl to solve real-world problems. Perhaps this fact best demonstrates the language's elegance.

Some people don't feel this way about Perl or even programming, and that's just fine: We (the authors) aren't artists, for that matter, which is why we didn't try to do the drawings for this book. That wouldn't have been fun. Sometimes we see people in this business who aren't motivated to explore or keep up their skills, and it's clear that they don't share the same love for it that we do. Our wish for them is that they find this passion somewhere, whether it's in this field

---

1. See Damian Conway's CPAN modules `Coy.pm` and `Lingua::Romana::Perligata` for quintessential examples of Fun with Perl.

or another; there's no dishonor in admitting that you've been a square peg in a round hole.

Some of the ways that people who have a love for Perl express it are

- Golf: Competing with others to see how few characters they can code a solution in.
- Bowling: Competing with others to see how long and arcane they can make the solution to a simple problem.
- Obfuscation: The archetypal track meet for this is the Perl Journal's annual contest at `http://www.tpj.com/contest.html`. The quintessential obfuscation vehicle is the JAPH, a piece of code which prints "Just another Perl hacker," albeit by the most impenetrable means possible.

If you love Perl too and are wondering where other people like you hang out, here are some suggestions:

- There are Perl Monger groups (local user groups) all over the world. Access the Web site `http://www.pm.org` to find the one nearest you, and pick up neat Perl accessories.
- The annual Perl conference run by O'Reilly & Associates takes place in the western United States in summer; see `http://conference.perl.com/`.
- There are annual alternatives in the eastern United States and Europe, both called YAPC (Yet Another Perl Conference), run by volunteers. See `http://www.yapc.org/America/` and `http://www.yapc.org/Europe/`.
- The Fun with Perl mailing list is a place for people to send short pieces of code that embody some really clever or elegant way of solving a problem. Frequently the list plays golf with them. See `http://www.technofile.org/depts/mlists/fwp.html`.

- A comprehensive listing of Perl mailing lists can be found at `http://lists.perl.org` and `http://www.perl.org/support/mailing_lists.html`.

- The `#perl` channel on IRC is inhabited by `purl`, an autonomous agent that has a revolving collection of knowledge about Perl and other things. Humans have been known to hang out there too; see `http://pound.perl.org/`. Suggestion: Spend some time observing the channel to see what's acceptable to the culture there before saying anything.

- A Perl portal with discussions, chat, and surveys can be found at `http://www.perlmonks.org`.

- A news-oriented Perl portal is at `http://use.perl.org`.

If you want to find out more about Perl from some less publicized angles, try:

- The history of Perl site at `http://history.perl.org/`.
- News on the development of Perl 6 at `http://www.perl.org/perl6/`.

14.3 This Really Is the End

We would like to leave the last word to Larry Wall. This is quoting him from the README file that comes with the Perl source code:

> Just a personal note: I want you to know that I create nice things like this because it pleases the Author of my story. If this bothers you, then your notion of Authorship needs some revision. But you can use perl anyway. :-)

> The author.

Appendix A

Perl Debugger Commands

"Follow the white rabbit."

Trinity in The Matrix

This appendix addresses the commands available in the Perl internal debugger as of version 5.6.0. It owes most of its content to the `perldebug` pod page and the debugger internal help screen.

A.1 General Syntax

The following apply to all commands entered in the debugger:

A.1.1 Continuation Lines

A line ending in a backslash (\) is concatenated with the next line before evaluation. No white space is permitted after the backslash.

A.1.2 Paging

`| command`

Run the debugger command, and pipe the debugger output through the current pager.

`|| command`

Run the debugger command, and pipe the program output through the current pager.

A.1.3 Command History

`! [n]`
`! pattern`

Run the command number *n* (default: previous command) or the last command that started with *pattern*. If *n* is negative, it is the *n*th command before the current one. The character can be changed from ! using the `recallCommand` option (discussed later).

```
H [-number]
```

You can display the last *number* commands with the H command.

Hitting the up and down arrow keys usually works to scroll through the command history. Only commands longer than one letter are put there.

A.1.4 Shell Interaction

```
!! command
```

Run *command* in a subshell. You can change the character from ! using the shellBang option (discussed later).

A.1.5 Command Aliasing

```
=[alias command]
```

Make *alias* an alias for *command*; then list all aliases. If omitted, just list all aliases. There is no way to clear aliases.

A.2 Commands

A.2.1 Help

```
h
h h
```

Get a verbose or concise help screen, respectively.[1]

```
h command
```

Get a line of help for the given debugger command.

---

1. It would be more accurate to say, a *concise* help screen and an *extremely concise* help screen, respectively.

`man` *page*

View the specified manual page. If your system doesn't have a `man` command, it uses `perldoc`; the command may be overridden by setting the variable `$DB::doccmd`.

A.2.2 Stopping or Restarting

`q`
`R`

The `q` command exits the debugger (so does end-of-file on the terminal). The `R` command attempts to rerun the program with the state changes you made preserved. Some state may be lost; breakpoints, history, actions, option settings, and the `-w`, `-I` and `-e` command-line options will be preserved.

A.2.3 Stepping

`n` *[expr]*
`s` *[expr]*
`<CR>`
`r`

`n` and `s` single step (over or into subroutine calls respectively). If *expr* is provided, then execute and step through that first. A carriage return by itself repeats the last `n` or `s`; if there wasn't one, it does nothing. `r` executes code until the last statement in the current subroutine.

A.2.4 Examining Package Data

`V` *[package [vars]]*
`X` *[vars]*
`S` *[[!]pattern]*
`m` *expr*

`V` lists variables in *package* (default: current package). *vars* can be a space-separated list. `X` is equivalent to `V` *current_package*. `S` lists subroutines that match (or with `!`, don't match) the given pattern.

Global variables like %ENV don't live in a particular package and thus won't be dumped with the V or X commands; use x instead.

m evaluates *expr* in list context and interprets the first element as either a class name or an object; it then prints the methods that can be called on it (the subroutines in its package and ancestor packages).

A.2.5 Examining Package or Lexical Data

p *expr*
x *expr*

p evaluates and prints *expr*. x evaluates (in list context) and dumps (in a Data::Dumper-style format) *expr*.

A.2.6 Showing Version Information

v

The v command shows the versions and source file locations of loaded modules.

A.2.7 Breakpointing

b *[point [condition]]*
b $var
c *[point]*

b sets a breakpoint before the location given (default: current line). c continues execution; if a location is given, it sets a one-time breakpoint there.

point is either a line number in the current file or a subroutine name (which is interpreted as the first executable line of that subroutine). Some lines are not breakable because they are not the start of executable code; perl gives an error if this is so. The subroutine has to have been compiled; for delayed loading, use the postpone form. If a variable $var evaluates to the name of or a reference to a subroutine, it can be used as a subroutine breakpoint.

condition is a perl expression to evaluate whenever the breakpoint is reached; the debugger will break only if it is true. Defaults to true.

```
b load filename
b compile sub
b postpone sub
```

The `load` form of *b* breaks when the given file is `required`. For subroutines that haven't been loaded yet, the `compile` form breaks when the given subroutine is compiled; the `postpone` form sets a breakpoint at the first executable line of the given subroutine.

```
d [line]
D
```

d deletes the breakpoint at the given line number (default: current line). There is no command to delete a breakpoint by subroutine name or to delete deferred breakpoints except for D, which deletes all breakpoints.

A.2.8 Actions

```
a [line [action]]
A
```

a causes the Perl code *action* to be executed whenever the given line number is reached (default: current line). If *action* is missing, delete any action set for the given line. A deletes all actions.

A.2.9 Action/Breakpoint Display

```
L
```

L lists all breakpoints and actions.

A.2.10 Stack Display

```
T
```

T displays the stack trace (a list of subroutines called on the way to the current line, with their respective arguments).

A.2.11 Source listing

```
l start+delta
l begin-end
l sub
l $var
l
-
```

List lines of source code: either the next *delta* lines from line number *start*, or from line *begin* to line *end*, or a window starting with the first line of a given subroutine or a variable that evaluates or points to one.

l by itself lists the next window following the one just displayed; – (minus) lists the previous window.

```
w [line]
.
```

w lists a window about the given line number (default: current line), and . (dot) resets the pointer for window listings to the current line.

```
f filename
/pattern/
?pattern?
```

f switches the file being viewed to the named file (which must be loaded), and *filename* must be either a full path or a regular expression that will match a loaded filename.

`/pattern/` and `?pattern?` move the pointer for window listings to the next (or previous) line matching the pattern.

A.2.12 Tracing

`t [expr]`

Set trace mode on (display lines as they are executed). If *expr* is supplied, execute and trace through it.

A.2.13 Watchpoints

`W [expr]`

Watch the variable (or lvalue indicated by) *expr*. When it changes, the debugger reports the old and new values and break. If *expr* is omitted, delete all watchpoints.

A.2.14 Prompt-Time Actions

`< command`
`< ?`
`<`
`<< command`

`< command` specifies perl code to be executed before each debugger prompt; `<< command` adds a command to the list. `< ?` lists the commands, and `<` by itself deletes them.

If you replace < with > in the previous list, you affect a separate set of commands to be executed after the debugger prompt.

If you replace < with { in the previous list, you affect a separate set of debugger commands (not Perl code) to be executed before the debugger prompt. There is no } counterpart.

A.2.15 Option Setting

Several internal switches can be changed to affect different states.

```
O  option
O  [option?]
O  option=value
```

An O command by itself lists all the current option settings; O *option*? lists the setting for that option. The option may be set to true (1) with the first command and to *value* with the last. More than one query or setting may be put on the line (space-separated) to affect multiple options at once. The list of possible options is in the next section. If an option value is a string containing spaces, put quotes around it.

A.2.16 Perl Code

Anything that does not fit into the previous categories is executed as Perl code in the DB package.

A.3 Options

When setting an option with the O command, it is necessary to type only enough initial letters to distinguish it from the other options. They are not case sensitive.

```
recallCommand
shellBang
```

Change the character used for command recall or shell escape respectively. Note in the case of the latter that it still has to be repeated; you are changing each ! , not the ! ! string.

`pager`

Set to | followed by the name of the program you want to use for paging; for example: `O pag='|less'`.

A.3.1 Options affecting the V, X, and x commands

`arrayDepth`
`hashDepth`

Set the maximum number of elements to print.

`quote`
`HighBit`
`undefPrint`

Change the style of string dumps. The valid values for quote are `"`, `'`, or `auto`.

`globPrint`

This is a Boolean indicating whether to print typeglobs.

`DumpDBFiles`
`DumpPackages`
`DumpReused`

These control whether to dump the contents of arrays holding debugged files, package symbol tables, and reused addresses, respectively.

`bareStringify`

If a variable overloads its stringify operator, don't call it; print the raw variable instead.

`usageOnly`

This causes V and X to display memory usage statistics for each package instead of listing variable values.

A.3.2 Options Affecting Exception Handling

```
signalLevel
dieLevel
warnLevel
```

By changing these values from their default of 0, you can get the debugger to intercept signals, warnings, and dies. With a value of 1, dies even within evals will be intercepted; with a value of 2, dies will be intercepted even if you created a $SIG{__DIE__} handler to trap them.

A.3.3 Options Affecting Control by Another Program

`RemotePort`

Specify a remote host and port number for remote control of the debugger in the format *host:port*.

`tkRunning`

Set if running under a PerlTk GUI.

`inhibit_exit`

According to the documentation, this controls whether the debugger allows "stepping off the end of the script," but it may be broken.

`immediateStop`

The debugger should "stop as soon as possible." If set in PERLDB_OPTS before invocation, debugging starts at the first line even if it is in a BEGIN block. This is handy for debugging used modules because normally the debugger will go past them before prompting.

A.3.4 Miscellaneous Options

```
compactDump
veryCompact
```

These affect the verbosity of the display of lists of lists.

```
frame
```

`frame` can be set to a number that is a combination of bit flags specifying certain information to be dumped whenever the stack frame changes (i.e., when a subroutine is entered or left). At the time of writing, some of the higher numbered flags had problems; we'll just say that `frame=1` shows subroutine entries and `frame=2` shows subroutine exits as well.

```
PrintRet
```

Set this option to false to inhibit printing of return information with the `r` command.

```
AutoTrace
```

This is the toggle set by the `t` command.

```
maxTraceLen
```

Used to set the maximum output used for argument printing in tracing.

```
ornaments
```

This affects display of the output.; see the `Term::ReadLine` package for value interpretations.

A.4 Environment Variables

The following environment variables affect the operation of the debugger:

PERL5DB

This contains the code that starts the debugger; if absent, it defaults to `BEGIN { require 'perl5db.pl' }`.

PERLDB_OPTS

This variable can contain initialization commands using options, which may, for instance, cause the debugger to run noninteractively and dump tracing information to a file. See the `perldebug` POD page for much more information.

PERLDB_RESTART

If this variable is defined, the debugger will then look for environment variables whose names begin with any of the following:

```
PERLDB_VISITED
PERLDB_HIST
PERLDB_ON_LOAD
PERLDB_POSTPONE
PERLDB_INC
PERLDB_FILE
PERLDB_OPT
PRELDB_PRETYPE
PERLDB_PRE
PERLDB_POST
PERLDB_TYPEAHEAD
```

This is how the debugger maintains state across restarts, and you should not change any of those variables. It would be fairly unlikely to do this by accident, of course.

PERLDB_NOTTY

This is used to specify a terminal to connect to after a noninteractive start. See the `perldebug` page for more information.

Appendix B

Perls of Wisdom

Aspirat primo Fortuna labori.

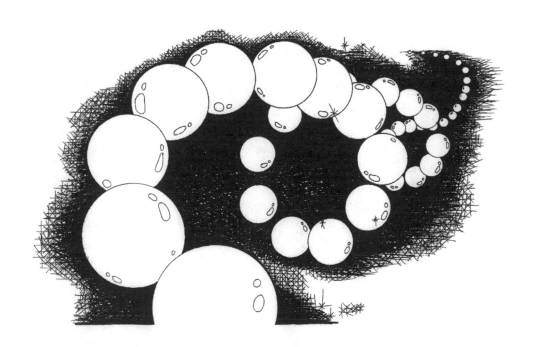

Index

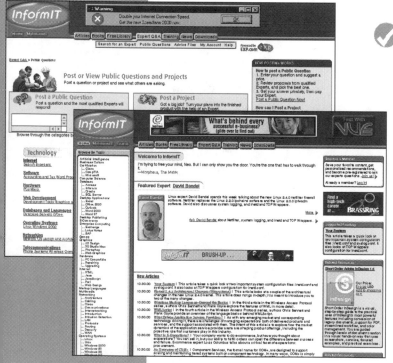

Perls of Wisdom

1 .... Know the documentation. Be able to find anything in it.

2 .... To get started with the perl documentation, type `perldoc perl`.

3 .... First know yourself; then your programs will be easier to know.

4 .... Motivate yourself by what you want to move *toward*, not what you want to get away *from*.

5 .... If you can't explain it to yourself or others, you won't be able to explain it in Perl.

6 .... Use a consistent style for each project.

7 .... Comment the hard parts. Use POD.

8 .... Declare as many of your variables as possible to be lexical.

9 .... Use `-w` and `use strict` in all your programs.

10 .... Use `use diagnostics` to explain error messages.

11 .... Create variables in the innermost scope possible.

12 .... If you have many explicit references to the same instance of `$_`, use a named variable instead.

13 .... When using a `while` loop that sets `$_`, localize `$_` first if it might be called from elsewhere.

14 .... Put empty parentheses after a function that could take arguments but doesn't.

15 .... Use parentheses when in doubt about precedence; they won't hurt.

16 .... Before testing the existence of a lower-level hash key, test the existence of the higher-level keys if there's a chance they may be absent.

17 .... Eliminate all causes of warning messages in a program before proceeding with further development.

18 .... Declare subroutines early, avoid collisions with the Perl built-in functions, or call them with `&`.

19 .... Don't pass arrays to built-in functions which normally expect a scalar.

20 .... Don't rely on loop variables retaining their values after the loop; save them explicitly if you need them.

21 .... Use the `Data::Dumper` module to print out a formatted dump of any variable or hierarchical data structure.

22 .... Migrate option setting to the most convenient input interface possible.

23 .... Use one-liners for rapid prototyping of small code constructs.

24 .... Examine references to hashes instead of the hashes themselves in the debugger to get well-formatted output.

From **Perl Debugged** by Peter Scott and Ed Wright   Addison-Wesley

Perls of wisdom

From **Perl Debugged** by Peter Scott and Ed Wright

Addison-Wesley